Pele's Wish

D1417070

Pele's Wish

Secrets of the Hawaiian Masters and Eternal Life

SONDRA RAY

Inner Ocean Publishing
Maui, Hawai'i • San Francisco, California

Inner Ocean Publishing
P.O. Box 1239
Makawao, Maui, HI 96768–1239
www.innerocean.com

©2005 by Sondra Ray
All rights reserved. No part of this book may be reproduced by any means or in any form whatsoever without written permission from the publisher.

Printed on recycled paper.

Cover design by Maxine Ressler
Book design by Madonna Gauding

PUBLISHER CATALOGING-IN-PUBLICATION DATA

Ray, Sondra.

    Pele's wish : secrets of the Hawaiian masters and eternal life / Sondra Ray. —Maui, Hawai'i : Inner Ocean, 2005.

        p. ; cm.

    Includes bibliographical references and index.
    ISBN: 1-930722-44-3

        1. Rebirthing. 2. Self-actualization (Psychology) 3. Spiritual healing. 4. Mental healing. 5. Health. 6. Childbirth—Psychological aspects. I. Title.

RZ403.R42 R39 2005
615.8/51--dc22   0504

Distributed by Publishers Group West

For information on promotions, bulk purchases, premiums, or educational use, please contact Special Markets: 866.731.2216

To my first *kahuna* teacher, Morrnah Simeona, who was always in tune with the frequency of the Most High and who always activated the sacredness of every soul she touched.

To Auntie Pua, who is always an opening for more light and things beautiful, and whose grace is moving through me and this book right now!

To Al and all the *kahuna* elders and helpers on all dimensions. May everything I am working on serve you and be infused with a higher cosmic destiny.

CONTENTS

Foreword   xi

Acknowledgments   xxi

Introduction   xxiii

Pele and the Sacred Vagina Cave   1

Goddess of Hawai'i's Volcanoes   11

Madame Pele's Wish   13

Balancing Masculine and Feminine   16

A Prayer to the Divine Mother for Peace and Balance   18

The Magic of the *Kahuna*   20

The Early *Kahuna* Initiations and Miracles   22

The Aloha Spirit and the Practice of Honoring the Other   23

Unique Principles Found in Huna Philosophy   30

The Secrets of Effective Prayer   38

The First Step before Prayer Is to Accumulate Extra *Mana*   40

The Ferson Method   41

Formula for Prayer Action   41

Understanding Blocks Between the Lower and Higher Self   43

Praise and Criticism   45

Example of Prayer for Relationship   46

Example of Prayer for Money   47

An Auspicious Meeting and Celebration   48

'Ohana Consciousness   52

Touching the Heart of the Islands   54

Morrnah's *Ho'oponopono* Teachings   58

Purpose and Use of *Ho'oponopono*   59

How *Ho'oponopono* Works with the Invisible Cords   62

Attitudes Required for *Ho'oponopono*   64

Conducting the Council   66

What It Might Look Like   69

Couples' Conflict Resolution the *Ho'oponopono* Way   71

The Power of *Ho'oponopono*   73

The *Kāhuna* and Healing   77

Powerful Philosophies of Healing   81

Opening the Blocks to Heal   83

Telepathy: Accessing Your Psychic Potentials   86

Changing Your Future   88

Lessons in Love   89

The Art and Science of Manifesting   91

Australian Spirituality   93

A Maori Healing, *Kahuna* Style   98

Spirituality in Everyday Life   100

Reflections on Immortality   101

Completing a Journey   105

    A Glossary of Terms in Native Hawaiian   108

    Annotated References   110

    References   113

    About Rebirthing   115

    About the Author   117

Foreword

I met Sondra Ray in 1996 when she contacted me to perform opening ceremonies and blessings for a spiritual seminar she was conducting in Maui. At that time, she had been coming to Hawai'i for several years, teaching spiritual development from the perspective of many traditions into which she'd been initiated over the years. In Hawai'i, she had learned much about the spiritual ways known here as "Huna." In 2002, after one of Sondra's seminars, she told me that she planned to go to the Big Island where she wished to visit the Vagina Cave. I told her that I needed to accompany her in that visit. Being a native Hawaiian, I had known about the caves all my life. My mother had first been told about them; she'd been taken to visit the caves and her ancestors there by her grandmother. As important as the Vagina Cave was to my family, I had never actually visited it. And so it seemed especially important to accompany Sondra and visit my ancestors, who I knew had resided there for hundreds of years.

Through my own family as well as spiritual training in the Huna tradition, I'd been taught that the Vagina Cave was identified with the goddess Pele, who most visitors to the island know only as the volcano by that same name. Few people know of Pele's origins, which are steeped in our native spiritual tradition. Long ago, in ancient Hawai'i, there were many gods and goddesses. They were known as "the chiefly flock of spirits," or *na pu'a ali'i 'uhane*. These spirits were found in all things in the heavens and in nature. One of these spirits was the goddess Hina, the supreme female spirit. She was also known as the mother of lesser gods, mother of humankind, patroness of fertility, and mother of the demigoddess Pele.

As soon as she became pregnant with Pele, Hina knew the child she was carrying would be different. And true to this expectation, a few days after the birth, Lonomakua, the keeper of the flame, looked into Pele's eyes and saw the reflection of fire. He knew this child would become the keeper of the fire that burned deep in the earth. She, Pele, would hold all the secrets of the fire and would one day rule all the volcanoes of Hawai'i. She would inherit the power to create and destroy land.

According to the ancient ones, when Pele came of age, the gods sent her on a journey with a canoe, *Honua-i-akea*. After many days at sea, she and her family arrived on an island that was completely unfamiliar to them. Great moun-

tains with a smoky haze hiding their peaks hinted of a volcano erupting. The smoky scent emitted by the volcanoes
was familiar to Pele. She thanked her father, Kanehoalani,
who had guided her to this place through the stars.

Many legends, often performed as dances, chants, and
songs, tell the story of Pele. The following is one that is
often quoted and sung:

No Kahiki mai ka wahine 'o Pele,
Mai ka 'aina mai 'o Polapola,
Mai ka punohu a Kane mai ke ao lapa i ka lani,
Mai ka 'opua lapa i Kahiki.

Lapaku i Hawai'i ka wahine 'o Pele,
Kalai i ka wa'a o Honua-i-akea,
Ko wa'a, e Ka-moho-ali'i, hoa mai ka moku,
Ua pa'a, ua 'oki, ka wa'a o ke akua,
Ka wa'a o kalai Honua-mea o holo.

From Tahiti comes the woman Pele,
From the land of Bora-Bora,
From the rising mist of Kane, dawn swelling in
    the sky,
From the clouds blazing over Tahiti.
Restless yearning for Hawai'i seized the woman
    Pele,

Built was the canoe, *Honua-i-akea,*
Your canoe, o *Ka-moho-aliʻi,* companion for voy-
    aging,
Lashed securely and equipped was the canoe of
    the gods,
The canoe for She-Who-Shapes-the-Sacred-Land
    to sail in.

When she arrived in at her destination, Pele joyfully
named the fire island "Hawaiʻi." With her magic fire stick,
Paʻoa, Pele came upon a large volcanic pit and named it
"Kīlauea." Inside this pit was a crater. She named it
"Halemaumau." Holding *Paʻoa* in her hand, Pele dedicated
the Kīlauea Volcano to her gods and declared the pit
Halemaumau as her home. *Pele-ai-honua,* Pele the eater of
the land, had arrived. Pele was home.

In the ancient stories of Pele, there are many teachings,
known as Huna, that are at the heart of the spiritual tradition of the islands. For me, going to the caves would be a
chance to visit my spiritual family, my sisters, brothers, and
all the old kings and queens of Hawaiʻi. They are blood to
me. This was an opportunity to spend time with my spiritual family, so this was a very joyous occasion.

The stories of Pele have been in my human family for
many years, so visiting my spiritual family in this way was
very real for me. When I was a child I learned that Pele

comes in many forms, even as an old woman at times. When my mother was a little girl, she was in her home with my great grandmother. My mother looked out the window and said, "Tutu, look, look! There's an old lady there, combing her hair." Her grandmother looked out. "Oh, that is Tutu Pele," she said. "There's going to be an eruption. Don't be afraid. It'll be fine." My mother noticed everyone else had left their homes. She and her family were the only ones there. "Tutu," she said, "we're the only ones here. We need to go."

Pele did erupt. My mother saw the lava coming down and went to her grandmother. Her grandmother said, "Don't worry, Haliaka, it's going to be okay." Sure enough the lava came down the hill, reached the stone wall, and went around it. When my mother looked out the window again, the old woman was gone. She told her grandmother, "Tutu, the lady is gone." And my great grandmother said, "Of course, Haliaka. I told you, it was Pele. Pele will always take care of us. She is part of the family. We are a part of *her* family."

Because of her great power, people tend to think that Pele is a destroyer. But she isn't. She will reclaim land that has been desecrated by humankind, but she always provides us with an opportunity to keep the balance. If we do not, then by all means Pele will reclaim that land. But she is not destroying; she is reclaiming and restoring.

As you will learn in the pages ahead, Pele is closely linked with the spiritual tradition of native Hawai'i. Madame Pele, as she is sometimes called, is the divine spark of creation and so she is an aspect of the Divine Mother, which we find in many other traditions the world over. The heart of this tradition is expressed in the word "aloha."

In time immemorial, the masters and teachers foresaw many changes coming, and so to keep the consciousness of those times, they placed the word in the language. When you listen to the Hawaiian language, it is very lyrical, very musical.

The word "aloha" holds the consciousness the ancients placed there: *"A"* (ah) is the first light of dawn, the spark of god, god the father, goddess the mother. *"Lo"* is the symbol and the sound of eternity, of forever. *"Ha"* is breath, the gift, the blessing of life that comes from God. And so, to say "aloha" is to remember our gift, what we have been given. It reminds us of our own inner greatness. We say, "Aloha ke Akua," God is love. "Aloha ke Akua," God is within us. "Aloha ke Akua," God is, I am. It is so simple, yet it is all there, within those teachings, teachings within teachings. Each step, each part, we must understand—God is love; God is within; God Is, I Am. Each step is a lesson, sometimes a very long lesson. It takes a long time to know each lesson. Sometimes you learn them only by living. Sometimes it is given to you in shared knowledge, in wisdom. How you get it depends on how you steer your life, how you live it.

"*Kahuna*" comes from the word "*huna*," referring to that which is hidden, or the mysteries. A *kahuna* is the keeper of that mystery, the teacher, if you will. As you begin to acknowledge the teachings and accept them as part of your life, and as you go through your life using the knowledge that has been given you, it ages well. That is what we call wisdom. This knowledge that we bring to our everyday lives goes toward becoming (be-come-in) wisdom.

There is a kind of internal rites of passage—one is initiated many times, by life, by light. Learning never stops, for a *kahuna* or anyone else. Graduation from different levels of knowledge and wisdom never ends. Teachings come from many sources. It might first come from the teacher within, the inherent wisdom we all have within us. That's part of it. Or it might come whenever you need it the most, maybe even from unexpected sources. When you are ready, the teacher appears. Teachers have always come. There is also the lineage, the tradition and history, the spoken story, the language. These are all important components of the wisdom as it is given to us. To do the work of the Huna, that is my *kuleana*, my responsibility.

It is my belief that wisdom is universal. Nobody has ownership of it; you get it through living your life. Everyone has something good to bring to the table, and that's where aloha comes in. In the practice of aloha, you learn to listen, you learn to discern, and what you want to accept you accept. If it feels good to you, it becomes your truth. Truth is truth. There's no right truth compared to others. Whether you agree or disagree, how you do it is called respect.

Everything is connected—the mineral and plant kingdom, the animal kingdom, which includes all creatures of the land, the sky and the ocean, and the human kingdom— each has its part of the whole, just like a family. When one of them leaves, the family is no longer complete. If the mineral kingdom was taken away, something would be missing in the greater scheme of life. Each kingdom comes with its own balance, and its balance is added onto the greater balance, the balance of the family, the balance of the universe. We're all linked. We're all in relation to one another.

Pele is like the housekeeper of our planet. When people say she is a destroyer . . . no! She is reclaiming the land. This is her *kuleana*, her responsibility. She is the menstrual cycle of our planet. Her release is through the ashes. She reclaims land that has been desecrated and with the flow of her lava she gives back new land. People have strayed away from understanding and remembering all about who she is.

In old Hawaiian society, several hundred years ago, they had the equivalent of what you see in modern society today. They had different experts, specialists, and practitioners of certain *kuleana* and responsibilities, so to speak.

Through the experiences we shared at the Vagina Cave, I came to see my friend Sondra not only as a spiritual seeker but as a genuine teacher who serves as a valuable bridge between cultures. Throughout her lifetime as a dedicated guide for many thousands of people, she has been able to bring to her students a rich perspective of the universality of spiritual wisdom. Through her comes a vision of how we are all truly linked as one and that each of us has direct access to the Divine through teachings that ultimately have no social or ethnic boundaries.

As I understand Pele's wish, it is a very simple message that we feel with our hearts—*to breathe, to live, and to be.*

—Puanani Mahoe

Acknowledgments

My mind is delighted in the counsel and grace of my main teachers Babaji, Jesus, *A Course in Miracles*, and Ammachi.

I also want to thank Inner Ocean Publishing and especially publisher Karen Bouris, and Hal Zina Bennett, my editor, who helped me and Auntie Pua deliver the vibes!

Introduction

I guess I was born a healer at some level because when my grandfather saw me at birth, he never went back to the mental institution. I also remember visiting the sick and poor people in our little town on my tricycle. It was inevitable, then, that when my father became ill and began going in and out of hospitals, my inclinations turned to studying nursing. I wanted to know why people in my town were getting sick and dying. Back then, we kids attended every funeral of every person who died in our neighborhood. School was even let out so that we could march the three miles out to the cemetery.

When I watched people I loved being put in the ground, I didn't understand why the church said, "The Lord took them away." I couldn't bear thinking that God killed people. So I started a mission early; I had to find out the truth about sickness and death. When my own father died the night before my graduation, and the whole town was crying when I gave a speech to accept my honors, you might say that was the final blow.

I rebelled against my family's religious leanings and married an atheist. But my desire to serve rose again when I heard President Kennedy make his famous speech about the Peace Corps. I told my husband we had to join. Unable to resist my enthusiastic zeal, he agreed and the two of us went through the very tough training. When we finally boarded the plane to Peru, we were told during take-off that President Kennedy had just been assassinated. We were numb. But there was no time to grieve when we landed, as Peru was suffering from an epidemic—the plague. The Peace Corps put me through a real boot camp for world service. I knew I would never be the same.

During graduate school I began to embrace my powers, which wreaked havoc on my marriage and ultimately left me divorced and devastated. I joined the Air Force Nurse Corps during the Vietnam War, but I was already so wounded that I just ended up in therapy.

One day my ex-husband called to say he wanted me back. I thought, maybe that is it. I should try again. I packed all my things and sent them to him in Florida.

But that night I had my first mystical experience. I was sitting on the floor talking to a friend about going back to my husband. All of a sudden we both heard a voice in the air. The voice said, "Never go back!" I was startled, but I could not get up and run. In fact, I couldn't move. Beams of light were holding me to the ground. The voice got louder and said, "Never go back! Go to California now!"

My friend looked at me and said, "Sondra, I think you better go to California."

I knew that if I didn't follow this voice I would regret it for the rest of my life. So I put together what was left of my belongings and was soon in my sports car heading for California, despite the letter from the Nurses' Association that said my master's degree didn't change the fact that there were no jobs available for nurses, despite being broke from a recent trip to Europe, and despite the unsettling thought of playing a wild card. I don't remember anything about the trip except that when I saw the California line, I started feeling really good. I turned the car toward San Francisco because of an article in *Time* magazine about someone doing medical research I was interested in.

The hills in San Francisco were scary, and I had no idea where I was going. But my car suddenly just quit on Scott Street, and my surname was Scott at the time. I looked up and saw a sign: "Furnished Apartment for Rent."

I knocked on the door of the *mana*ger's apartment.

"I need to live here," I said.

"Ma'am," he said, "you need the first month's rent, the last month's rent, and the cleaning deposit." He added up the sum. There was no way I could afford it. But I kept telling him I needed to live there, and I simply could not move my body away from him.

I think he was shocked at my persistence. Finally he said, "Lady, I don't know what it is about you, and I have never done this in twenty-five years, but you can move in."

I promised him I would get a job. The next day I found the researchers I'd read about in *Time* magazine, who told me that although they had no funding to hire me, they could make a call to help me find a job. Lo and behold, I landed a job at Kaiser Hospital in Oakland, in spite of what the Nurses' Association had written me. The job was a miracle. I was in charge of an OB-GYN clinic. It was the perfect preparation for my career to come.

The hairdresser on my block told me about the latest thing in San Francisco—a training called EST. So I took a few workshops there, which opened me up a lot. Unfortunately, I was in a series of car accidents after that. I was always getting my sports car banged up on the left rear, whether I was driving it or it was just parked. I had my car in the shop so often that it began to affect my commute to work.

One night I was crying over this in a graduate seminar. Three guys came up to me and asked what was wrong. I told them I was in a *syndrome*. They said, "Don't worry. There is this new guru in town."

I was willing to try anything. My hair was still falling out from my divorce, I had a lot of pain in my body, and now I was getting into car accidents.

The next Sunday morning, my three new friends drove me to the mountains near San Jose. There was a man standing on a hill with about twenty people around him. He was talking about what he called the "Five Biggies in Life," which turned out to be the five most negative thought structures that keep people from being in bliss. They are:

1. Birth trauma

2. Specific negative thought structures

3. The parental disapproval syndrome

4. The unconscious death urge

5. Influences from other lifetimes

I knew the cause of my problems was somewhere in that list, and I definitely had not handled whatever it was. So I said, "This man is my teacher." The man's name was Leonard Orr.

On another occasion he came to an astrology class I was attending and said, "Who wants to try this new thing?" My hand was in the air, and I don't remember putting it up because I didn't even know what I was volunteering for. Leonard said, "Okay, you. You have to drop out for a week and come with me."

How could I do this when I had just started a new job with no immediate vacation time? It *seemed* impossible, but then again, so had finding an apartment and a job, so I thought maybe I would be lucky again. I went to the head of Kaiser Hospital and told him I needed a week off for my spiritual development. I think he was so taken aback that he didn't even realize he was saying yes. Well, destiny is destiny. Suddenly the whole universe was cooperating.

Leonard took about ten of us out to the woods. One by one we got into a redwood hot tub with him, rolled up in the fetal position, and breathed a certain way through a snorkel. This was my first "rebirthing session," as he called it. After the tub, I was carried to a place under a tree. I looked up and saw the aura around all the leaves. I had never seen auras before. Something big was going on here.

I mustered up all my self-esteem and the next day asked Leonard, "How do I become a rebirther?"

"Handle your own birth trauma and move in with me."

All I'd known about my birth until then was that Mom always said I came straight from the kitchen. She loved the fact that I was born on the kitchen table. I, on the other hand, did not think it was so great since I have been traumatized by food ever since.

Home births were not common when I was born, so the whole town, population three hundred, showed up to see me. Mom says even people from other towns came to check me out. I'm not sure why, but maybe that was the beginning of my being a public figure. I never had any intention of being a public figure, but even as a child I was pretty sure I was supposed to be a missionary. For a while I wanted to be a stewardess, but I was too tall.

As I worked on my rebirthing, guided by Leonard, the awareness of my birth expanded and grew. Leonard got a big old house in the Haight Ashbury region of San Francisco. The house had a very racy history, having been a drug haven as well as anything else you can think of. A bunch of us who were enthralled with Leonard's new breathing technique moved in with him. We had no furniture but soon we had a hot tub in the basement. Every day, I would come home after work and we would all rebirth each other. Our lives began to change drastically. I suddenly realized that the reason I had had so many bang-ups on the left rear of my car was because that was where the doctor had hit me at birth!

The good news was that all the pain went out of my body, my hair grew back, I started having really good relationships with men, and I felt fantastic. I was beginning to realize it was my destiny to become a spiritual healer. One day, I realized it was crazy to give pills and perfect nursing care to patients when they would only get sick again. How was it that the people getting rebirthed were experiencing permanent healing just by this special breathing technique and changing their thoughts? Pretty soon I gathered up all my courage and left medicine. It was scary but I knew we were onto something really big.

I began to notice something phenomenal in my rebirthing practice. Clients would come to me and tell me *all* of their problems, especially those about sex and relationships. Then I would give them another session and they would have a memory of their birth. I was stunned to see how discovering what happened during their birth affected their relationships in very negative ways. I began to keep this data in my head.

One day Leonard told me to go to Hawai'i and teach a seminar. This was a new experience for me. I didn't know what to say, so all I did was share my experiences with rebirthing. The day went by really quickly, and everyone's mouths were hanging open. They said, "Sondra, this explains everything! You have to stay, and we want to bring our friends tomorrow."

Their friends had the same reaction to my seminar. They were amazed at how much was explained about their lives. I went back to San Francisco and wrote down as much as I could about what I had experienced in Hawai'i. These writings grew to become what I called "The Loving Relationships Training." News about the seminar spread like wildfire, and suddenly I was out there, traveling and teaching.

I began writing books and soon was invited to speak in

foreign countries. I never spoke on TV then because we didn't have enough rebirthers trained. Soon I could not keep up with demand alone, so I had to quickly train other rebirthers and other trainers. The Loving Relationships Training was a huge success for over ten years.

Then we were called to India. Things would never be the same again. When we found our master, Babaji, it was so thrilling and so shocking to our system that no words can ever convey the supreme glory or extreme challenge of it.

Try to imagine meeting a being, not born of a woman—yes, that's right, someone who did not come through the birth canal. This master had materialized his body in a ball of light in a cave. When you were with him, he knew every single thing about your past, present, and future.

He could totally liberate you, if you were willing. Suddenly he was pushing me to be great. He was changing my DNA, smashing my ego to smithereens. He was showing me infinite possibilities, activating all my past lives to be cleared. He was giving me more unconditional love than I could have ever imagined. He was downloading the kingdom of God in my very apartment, demonstrating to me a living revelation of the life force. He was breaking me out of all old paradigms. He was giving me a life of divine creativity. He was vibrating with the Christ Presence right before my eyes, shaking me to the roots. He was making me face all the darkness in me, all while giving me constant divine inspiration.

He arranged constant *"lilas"* (divine plays of the guru to crack your case) for me to go through to clear my karma. He showed me miracles that blew my mind and made me leave behind the old way that I'd lived my life. He was giving me a life of awe and wonder as quickly as I could take it in. He twisted my consciousness and made me go to the depths of my being. He offered me a cosmic reality of what life could be like and shook out every disturbance in my mind. He made my problems disappear. His grace allowed me to begin to rejoice in my life. He was making me an ambassador for the eternal while I shook in fear, releasing all my death programming. He saturated my soul with his essence while keeping me just far enough away so I would not burn up.

He surrounded me with beautiful yogis and Hawaiian *kahuna* who I've written about in this book. And one day I realized that he had been the voice in the air that day, the one that told me to "never go back." He turned my life around. He had been guiding me all along, and he was in charge of my evolution. My old life fell apart completely; I was no longer who I thought I was. And so it was that my attention began to focus on the presence of God, moment by moment, and life became a continuous celebration. The same is available to all.

I began taking groups to the Himalayas, and my work accelerated at such a speed that I had to scramble to complete the assignments Babaji gave me. Even now he pushes me to advance and deconstruct and reconstruct myself. He has thrown me into the arms of the Divine Mother. She has won my heart and placed me in the field of the miraculous. I also became a devotee of Ammachi, who is in fact also in Christ Consciousness and somewhat like electric shock therapy.

And never do they let up on me. Just when I think I am cruising, they force me into a higher vibe and remind me why I am here—to change fear to love, death to life.

Om Namaha Shiva Jai Ma!

Pele and the Sacred Vagina Cave

I was inside the Vagina Cave on the island of Hawai'i when I received the assignment to do this project. This particular cave was somewhere outside of Hilo on the Big Island. It was not open to tourists, and only those who knew about it or could get a reliable guide ever found their way to it. Thousands of lava tubes form these caves. Some were used as burial caves. Some larger chambers were used as hospices for the ill and dying. Some were hiding places during battles. In this huge cave, Madame Pele, goddess of fire, had carved out tubes and caverns that actually resembled female parts.

I was there with Auntie Pua, a spiritualist in the *kahuna* tradition of Hawai'i, and she was having ongoing visions of the Hawaiian elders. At the entrance to the caves, she chanted in Hawaiian, seeking and finally receiving permission to enter. She told me we were being led in by a group of warriors, who were in front of, on the sides of, and behind us. I could not see them, but I knew what she said was true.

We went in through the ovary, crawled down the fallopian tube, then went into the womb. Our guide knew exactly what she was doing. When we found the spot we wanted, I laid out some koa leaves for an altar and lit some candles.

Auntie Pua described what she was seeing—a gathering of the ancients: "They want you to be the ambassador of aloha," she told me. "Pele is holding you in her bosom."

I began to weep softly and deeply. I was so touched and so honored. Mind you, we were sitting inside the uterus at the time.

Auntie Pua said the chiefs and "chiefesses," kings and queens, knew I could write and wanted the truth out and told with integrity. They all honored Pele. And who wouldn't upon seeing Pele's manifestations on the Big Island of Hawai'i?

Pele is about fire, passion, and life itself. She is one of a host of powerful and revered gods and goddesses of Hawai'i.

Auntie Pua described what she was seeing—a gathering of the ancients: "They want you to be the ambassador of aloha," she told me. "Pele is holding you in her bosom."

People stand in awe of the fire flowing down the mountainside, watching Pele create new land.

As goddess of the volcanoes, it is impossible to imagine Hawai'i without Madame Pele. I feel so alive when I think of her, and I just want to be in her good favor. How perfect it would be to serve her in the way I'd been asked. The elders wanted me to be passionate about expressing aloha—to get everyone passionate about expressing aloha. What better assignment could I be blessed with? It felt like the Eternal Fountain of Love (aloha) showering blessings on me.

After I agreed to the assignment and the elders had left, we crawled out the other fallopian tube and out the other ovary and came upon the vulva. There it was, clitoris and everything. Now, you have to imagine it all in extra large sizes. The vulva was perfect in shape and everyone obviously treated it as a sacred altar. Flowers and gifts were placed next to it. I was in awe of the way Madame Pele had fashioned the whole thing, as if consciously done and planned perfectly.

The cave was huge. At the beginning of one tunnel, the guide cautioned us not to go in. She said it was a lava tube so long that some people

> The vulva was perfect in shape and everyone obviously treated it as a sacred altar . . . . I was in awe of the way Madame Pele had fashioned the whole thing, as if consciously done and planned perfectly.

walked for two-and-a-half weeks but had to turn back when they ran out of water.

Spelunking had been a hobby of mine in college, but I hadn't done it much since I found the cave I had been secretly looking for—Babaji's cave in the foothills of the Himalayas where he had materialized his body. I have visited that cave every year since my first visit and had lost interest in all other caves until I heard about Hawai'i's Vagina Cave. I was lucky to hear about this place since, as far as I know, it has not been advertised anywhere.

I found out about the cave during a boat trip on Maui that I'd taken with the intention of watching whales. The whales and dolphins were not the only highlight of the trip—the company on the boat was very special as well. Three great healers were there: Howard Wills, Bunji (a great aboriginal crystal healer), and Bhagvandas (a great spiritual musician). The other people on the boat had received healings from them. I was really happy to be asked to join them at the last minute. I knew the three of them had traveled through the islands, and as I sat with Bhagvandas, we struck up a conversation. I asked him to tell me the highlight of his tour on the islands.

"Without a doubt," he said, "it was the Vagina Cave on the Big Island."

As he told me of his amazing experiences I knew I had to go there. Many months before I went to the Hawaiian

Islands, my spiritual guide informed me that I would write a book that would rock the world. She gave me no additional information. I had decided then and there that I would go where the rocks were being formed by the volcanic activity of Madame Pele.

I spent all of December on Maui getting in the Hawaiian aloha spirit. I taught a few seminars, each time having a *kahuna* open them, which is traditional in the islands. At one seminar, Auntie Pua stayed on stage with me the entire time. This was unusual. It was as if she knew I had to build up a lot of Hawaiian energy. This was ecstasy for me. Auntie Pua moved the energy in a way that was perfect for all of us.

One day I mentioned to Auntie Pua that I had to go to the Big Island, and she said she had to go with me. I was stunned. "You would go with me?" I blurted out, surprised that I could be so lucky.

"Yes," she said. "I have to properly introduce you to the volcano."

I was told that the active volcano on the Big Island is considered to be the living body of Madame Pele. I was more than ecstatic to be going there with her. I ran along the beach shouting "Ja Ma!" (victory to the Divine Mother). This was an expression I'd learned during my previous pilgrimages to India, where I had also learned about the teachings of the Divine Mother.

I told my assistant to get me two tickets to the Big Island and that I had to be there New Year's Day. My assistant reported there were no seats available at all—it was already nearly New Year's Eve. I told her we simply had to go and she must keep trying. She came back a little while later and announced that no small planes were available either. I told her to keep trying. After making many calls, she was finally able to reroute us back to Honolulu and over to Hilo.

It was not a problem that Auntie Pua and I did not have a car for getting around the island. As we talked over dinner everything just came to us. We didn't even have to ask for what we needed out loud.

We sat very still at dinner that evening. Among the people who came to our table to say hello and welcome us was someone who offered to drive us the top of the volcano—exactly where we wanted to go. All we needed was a guide who could take us to the caves. And who should approach us but a woman who does sacred dance and she offered to be our guide.

Though I was in awe of our fortune, Auntie Pua acted as though nothing was out of the ordinary and always treated me as a *kahuna* myself. Never had I mentioned to her that clairvoyants had told me I was a *kahuna* in past lives. She just knew.

Months later I'd reflect that my life really was getting

easier and easier, and things were finally coming to me, but not quite as they had during that visit with Auntie Pua by my side. With the two of us together, the whole island seemed to be of service. That was real aloha.

> Imagine this: you are driving along and the road just turns into cooled lava, and you wonder why it stopped right there.

At five the next morning, still in the dark, we traveled to the top of the volcano, as far as we could go in the car. The lava, which had been running down the road, had stopped suddenly and cooled. Imagine this: you are driving along and the road just turns into cooled lava, and you wonder why it stopped right there.

We began hiking over the cooled lava, which is a bit like walking on the moon. We were walking on a trail around the edge of the Kīlauea Volcano, whose crater is twelve hundred feet deep and more than two miles in circumference.

While walking on the cooled lava flows, we crossed shiny expanses of black lava, with occasional steam vents that interrupt the desolation. There were lava cones, as well as cinders, like peaks and craters, with jagged, rough lava, black but dusted with specks of gold, silver, and blue. We hiked for what seemed like several hours until we got as close as we could to where the red-hot moving lava was still spilling down into the ocean. Steam rolled up hundreds of feet from the sea. The energy in this place was mind blowing.

Auntie Pua announced that she wanted to perform a ritual to purify and ground me in preparation for going to the Vagina Cave. She picked a cool spot for me to lie down. Then she chanted in Hawaiian, prayed and fanned me with ti leaves. When she was done, we hiked back to the car. Little did I know what was to come the next day.

After the ritual I thanked Auntie Pua and we set out to find the Vagina Cave and go in together. We had no idea where the cave actually was. The only information we had was that it was on the Hilo side of the island, which is why I considered it lucky that the only place we could find a hotel on short notice happened to be on the Hilo side of the island.

Auntie Pua confessed to me that, being from Maui, she had never been to the Vagina Cave herself. I was really happy because I felt we would both be experiencing this treat together. With the help of a guide we found the opening to the cave. The

With the help of a guide we found the opening to the cave. The entrance was overgrown with vegetation and hidden from the view of anyone unfamiliar with its location. And so it was that we were able to visit the cave where the elders would ask me to be the ambassador of aloha.

entrance was overgrown with vegetation and hidden from the view of anyone unfamiliar with its location. And so it was that we were able to visit the cave where the elders would ask me to be the ambassador of aloha.

The day after our visit to the Vagina Cave, we were invited to a private residence known as Shangri-La. There was an incredible lagoon in the backyard, about as big as three swimming pools. It was warm and the bottom was all lava. I got in and began doing wet breathwork with my snorkel. I started thinking about this book and really wanted to know what it would be about. I prayed for a title but nothing happened. I kept on breathing with all my determination. A woman swam over to me and asked if I would like a Watzu session, which is a form of transformative body work performed in the water.

I said, "Are you kidding?" She wasn't.

Nothing could have been better at that moment. I got so relaxed during the session. Soon I heard the words "Pele's wish." I was thrilled because I knew it was to be the title of this book.

I was not at all sure what Pele's wish might be, but I figured that if this aspect of the Divine Mother could manifest volcanoes, she knew what she was doing and someday she would tell me more about her wish.

After our experiences at the Vagina Cave and Shangri-La, Auntie Pua returned to Maui. I stayed to continue my

> Pele personifies what Auntie Pua had described as the life force, or divine creativity, and is one of the ancestral spirits, the goddess of volcanoes.

work. The journey had been an adventure for me, one that took me very deep, literally and figuratively.

Pele personifies what Auntie Pua had described as the life force, or divine creativity, and is one of the ancestral spirits, the goddess of volcanoes. Some native Hawaiians, as well as others who come to the islands, feel they have a personal relationship with her. To this day many see her and refer to her, in a familiar way, as Tutu Pele, or Madame Pele.

Since Pele is known for her passion and sensuality, she is sometimes seen as the epitome of a vibrant woman. Without Pele, the islands themselves would not exist. She created the land by bringing up her great flow of red-hot magma from the deep core of Mother Earth. Even Mauna Loa, a large volcano on the Big Island, is believed to have been created by Pele.

Goddess of Hawai'i's Volcanoes

Madame Pele is a source of great inspiration and supernatural power. It is believed that even the tiniest rock she creates contains quantities of *mana,* the sacred energy source so important to the *kāhuna* for spiritual transformation and healing.

Pele's traditional home is the active crater Halemaumau at the Kīlauea Volcano on the Big Island, now embodying one of the most splendid U.S. national parks. It is believed that she can appear as an old hag or a sensuous young woman, beautiful, majestic, and mysterious. The many ancient legends about her reveal an impetuous, lusty, and mysterious nature. At times gentle and loving, she is also unpredictable, capable of sudden fury and great violence.

> It is believed that even the tiniest rock she creates contains quantities of *mana,* the sacred energy source so important to the *kāhuna* for spiritual transformation and healing.

There are photos taken of volcanoes erupting in which a woman's face has shown up in the middle of the fire and smoke! This, it is said, is Madame Pele. I saw this picture myself at the Volcano House. The Divine Mother takes many forms.

Several times I have been in helicopters looking at the red lava below. I wish everyone could see that just once. To witness new land being created right before your eyes, and from the source, does something magical to the beholder. For one thing, it gave me such gratitude for this continual demonstration of the constancy of the life force. It allowed me to understand immortality at a much deeper level than ever before, for here was a demonstration of it, with new land emerging from within the earth. It made me respect and appreciate all the people living on the island who could handle such raw energy without going crazy . . . especially the Hawaiian people who knew how to show respect for Pele.

It would be wonderful if more tourists could really take the time to stay and experience the spiritual feelings that arise on the island. In that helicopter, I wondered if people really felt awe about the mystery of life, if they felt "in the presence of the breath of life," if they experienced the meaning of aloha. It all made me love life more, which generated more passion for all that life has to offer. It made me want to get more in harmony with life itself. It renewed my desire to live on and on.

Madame Pele's Wish

Madame Pele is an eternal spark of creation, an expression of the unconditionally loving and divine feminine. She wants us to be healed, to be empowered and whole, balanced and harmonious in all of our relationships. She sees us as priests and priestesses furthering the evolution of spirit within humanity.

Throughout the world there is the concept of the Divine Mother, who appears in many forms. She is the powerful, loving, and creative force of the universe. For me, Pele is an expression of this force, the paradigm shifter, the midwife for us all. She longs for us to learn from her the skills to regenerate our cells, to heal our lives and celebrate life in the highest ecstasy. I feel her longing to expand our awareness and innate capacities and activate the Christ Codes in our bodies. As an expression of the Divine Mother, the intelligence behind matter, she

> Madame Pele is an eternal spark of creation, an expression of the unconditionally loving and divine feminine. She wants us to be healed, to be empowered and whole, balanced and harmonious in all of our relationships.

longs to give us the solutions to all the problems we face.

Will we listen?

Now is the time for empowerment. Are you ready? Are you willing to hold the grail cup of the Divine Mother?

Madame Pele's wish is that we would all be in service to life.

Madame Pele's wish is that we would remember who we really are.

Madame Pele's wish is that we would each become emissaries of pure love.

Madame Pele's wish is that we would enter the state where miracles occur easily and effortlessly and are a part of our everyday reality.

Madame Pele's wish is that we would achieve self-mastery.

Madame Pele's wish is that we would see life as a passage of initiation and treat it with supreme reverence.

Madame Pele's wish is that we would open ourselves to our wisdom and support spiritual evolution and beauty on this planet.

Madame Pele's wish is that we allow the Divine Mother to express through us so that we may always uplift life.

When I speak of the Divine Mother, I am referring to the original spark of creation, which is a feminine aspect. The prime creator behind all things is a feminine vibration.

The Divine Mother is the feminine aspect of God, the intelligence behind matter. Einstein knew this. All my male gurus in India who perform miracles know this. It is the secret of their power. This is true power: love, safety, and certainty. It is not ego power, which is about domination, control, and anger.

The great Saint Sri Aurobindo said that the final stage of perfection is surrender to the Divine Mother. In India they say that there is nothing higher than worship of the Divine Mother. The Divine Mother vibration needs to be emphasized now as never before in all of history, since we can see from the results of human actions all around the world that we are out of balance. The sacred feminine has been suppressed for so long that we have lost touch with our true essence.

The following prayer expresses the surrender Sri Aurobindo speaks of:

My Queen, my Mother, I give thee all myself and to you my devotion to thee, I consecrate to thee my eyes, my ears, my mouth, my heart, my entire self. Wherefore, oh, Loving Mother, as I am thine own, keep me, defend me as thy property and possession. Oh, Divine Mother, you are in charge not me.

Balancing Masculine and Feminine

In each of us there is a masculine and feminine side. Being out of balance, we are addicted to the masculine side; thus, chauvinism runs rampant. Men and women have both been taught to equate masculinity with domination and violence. This problem is accentuated in many religious dogmas. The model of the universe in which a wrathful male God rules the cosmos serves to support male dominance in many of our social institutions.

We cannot merely reject systems that aren't working. They must be replaced. Nor would it work to replace our present patriarchy with a matriarchy. That will not even be allowed. However, throughout history, when the Divine Mother was worshipped by both men and women, and where both ruled together as equals, there has been peace. No one dominated anyone.

When people surrender to the Divine Mother, extraordinary changes take place. To explore the goddess energy is to truly value and embrace life. The Divine Mother is the source of all knowledge, beyond everything, and it is through her wisdom that we can all be released from delusion. This essence of the life force *(Shakti)* cannot be controlled. The Divine Mother, expressed as *"kundalini,"* will clean you out. Your old personality becomes replaced by miracle consciousness. The greater your devotion to her, the faster your progress. Through her we can achieve true happiness.

Everything we possess is a gift from the Mother. When we surrender to her, the intelligence of the whole universe becomes our teacher. We feel within us an urge to manifest even the inexpressible and invisible, bring it into the world as form and matter. We suddenly remember the ecstasy of being alive. Our bodies then become instruments through which the feminine aspect plays.

Through the Divine Mother men can learn to be more sensitive and intuitive, and women can learn to thrive in their own power. Are you, for example, a woman who grew up pleasing rather than being? Do you do almost anything to avoid a man's irritation? Have you immersed yourself in the values of a male-dominated society? Did you reorder your priorities and give your power away just to please a man? Wouldn't you rather be a fully awakened woman with a balanced feminine and masculine side? The more balanced you are the deeper your relationships can be with all human beings.

Are you a man who is afraid to feel his feelings, afraid to show softness and tenderness? Do you feel pressured into becoming a money-making machine? Are you afraid to give up your anger for fear of becoming weak? (Did you know that anger weakens every cell of your body?) Wouldn't you rather become a fully awakened male who is in balance, who could easily channel the right solutions for the world and provide the right environment for physical, emotional, mental, and spiritual progress?

Oh, Divine Mother, teach us to surrender to you totally so that we can move forward with bringing the masculine and feminine energies together, to manifest peace, love, and respect for everything that exists on our planet.

A Prayer to the Divine Mother for Peace and Balance

Peace, peace upon all the earth. May all escape from ordinary consciousness and be delivered from attachment. May they awaken to the knowledge of thy divine presence, unite themselves with thy supreme consciousness, and taste the plenitude of peace that springs from it.

Divine Mother, thou art the sovereign governess of One Being. Thy law is our law and with all our strength we aspire to identify our consciousness with thy eternal consciousness.

Oh, that we may accomplish thy sublime work in each thing and at every moment deliver us from the ordinary outlook on things. Grant that we may henceforth see only with thine eyes and act only by thy will.

Transform us into living torches of thy divine love, with reverence and with devotion and in joyful consecration of our whole being, we give ourselves, oh, Divine Mother, to the fulfillment of the law.

The Magic of the *Kāhuna*

Did you know that in ancient times, *kāhuna* practiced a magic that enabled them to control the weather, easily foresee the future, heal the sick instantly, and even raise the dead? Did you know that they kept the sharks from biting people? Did you ever wonder how they were able to do this magic? Wouldn't you like to know this magic for yourself?

The laws that worked for the *kāhuna* two hundred years ago continue to be given respect and great interest today. But you need to understand Huna to make use of them. Huna is not really a religion so much as it is spiritual practice. It is a name given to the wisdom the *kāhuna* practice in their everyday lives. It is a philosophy of achievement, meaning that it is judged by what it achieves in your daily life. In Hawaiian, the term *"kahuna"* means "that which is hidden, not obvious." It refers to hidden knowledge or secret reality, that which is difficult to see on the surface. A *kahuna,* then,

> In Hawaiian, the term *"kahuna"* means "that which is hidden, not obvious." It refers to hidden knowledge or secret reality, that which is difficult to see on the surface.

is a man or woman who is in touch with this knowledge. In the past it took approximately two decades for a person to become a *kahuna*.

Originally, the word *"kahuna"* was used to describe someone who belonged to an order that practiced and taught this knowledge. The *kāhuna* were and are spiritual leaders, master artists and craftsman, doctors, lawyers, teachers, and political advisors who draw upon this wisdom in their work in the world.

Language was particularly important to the ancient *kāhuna* since they kept the secrets of their practice hidden in it. The code system in the Hawaiian language is very powerful, for it reaches even into our cellular memories. (The original Hawaiians had no negative words in their language. Imagine that!) Breaking down the word "Hawai'i" reveals the following: *"ha"* means breath, *"wai"* means water, and the last *"i"* is the spirit in you and me. So Hawai'i is of the highest spirit/breath/light and life.

Auntie Pua told me that the state motto is rooted in the fact that the life of the land is perpetuated in righteousness, meaning the right, appropriate, and proper use, which applied to everything in the world. She said the land includes the embodiment of wisdom, and since everything is connected, misusing the land disrupts the balance of all. "The elements are teachers to us," Auntie Pua said. Just as the land embodies the culture and its wisdom, the wind represents the breath, the water represents the emotions, and the fire represents the movement of spirit.

Auntie often talked to me about the passion for the sheer joy of living. Her mind is unlimited. When I spoke to her of my beliefs about immortality, she explained that many *kāhuna* understood immortality from the viewpoint that the soul is immortal. Our souls live forever, *kau a kau,* from season to season. She also relates to physical immortality. The *kāhuna* were and are unlimited, and we have much to learn from them. So then, let's breathe, relax, and open our hearts and minds to their teachings.

The Early *Kahuna* Initiations and Miracles

You might think that Jesus was the only one who ever raised people from the dead. But the *kāhuna* had no problem matching this. One *kahuna* told me that when an elder *kahuna* was ready to pass the knowledge to one chosen to receive it, the final test, or initiation, was for the student to drink poison. If he died from it, he flunked. If he lived, he could carry on the tradition. "However," my friend assured

me, "in modern times, the teacher would have more compassion and resurrect the dead student." I knew he was
telling me the total truth and that he had in fact seen it as he
said. After all, what *kahuna* would want the karma of lying?

The Aloha Spirit and The Practice
of Honoring the Other

Before I go into depth about the Huna philosophy, I want
to welcome each of you by saying "Aloha!" I honor you for
choosing to read this book so that you, too, can learn to create your own magic in the *kahuna* tradition. The path to
this knowledge begins with language and the teachings that
are held by many Hawaiian words.

In the Hawaiian language, *"alo"* means bosom, in the
sense of taking something to heart or fully embracing it with
your heart. It also means the center of the universe. *"Ha"* is
the breath of God. Therefore, "aloha" refers to a feeling, a
recognition of the Divine. It can also mean "in the presence
of Divine Breath." It has many meanings. The simplest and
most basic translation of "aloha" is love. It can also refer to
kindness, unity, agreeableness, humility, and patience.

In the Hawaiian language, *"alo"* means bosom, in the sense of taking something to heart or fully embracing it with your heart. It also means the center of the universe. *"Ha"* is the breath of God. Therefore, "aloha" refers to a feeling, a recognition of the Divine.

Aloha evokes a spirit of grace, warmth, and connection between people. It can mean anything heartfelt, from deep personal love to mercy, kindness, compassion, and brotherhood. Auntie Pua also told me that *"a"* is the light of dawn, the first light, the spark that greets you each day. We are the *"a,"* we are the spark. So when we greet another by saying "Aloha!" we are saying, "I greet all the light that is within you with all the light that is within me."

Auntie Pua also told me that the *"lo"* of "aloha" represents the eternal, and *"ha"* refers to the breath of God, spirit, or the *mana* that comes forth from God. When we say "Aloha!" we acknowledge that God has breathed life into us, our own spirits being the light that is forever blessed by God. *Mana* is power. So you could say that the aloha that each of us holds and represents is the light forever blessed by spirit.

When used as a greeting, "aloha" extends sympathetic feelings of good will, with the intention of creating bonds of affection. On a higher level, it is the ideal toward which we strive in all relationships, a sharing from the heart in a spirit of generosity and peacefulness. My favorite definition is this: "The eternal spark forever between us." And that brings me exactly to my goal here—for you to feel the eternal spark forever between us. Let the rain of blessings fall!

We soon begin to see that the essence of the *kahuna* teachings might be summed up as loving ourselves, nurturing all other beings, including the land, and living in harmony with all of life. It is knowing that everything in the universe responds to love and kindness. And it means not just *knowing* but *practicing* this knowledge at all times.

From ancient times, the *kāhuna* were always able to see the big picture. They have always been tuned in to the larger universe, embracing the rocks, ocean, birds, land, people, plants, insects—in short, all that exists. They saw and were in touch with the energy that united everything in the universe. They knew that these forces must be kept in harmony. It was obvious to them that when one fosters and maintains a reverence for life, life responds in the same way. They always acknowledged that we live in a spiritual universe governed by spiritual laws.

The *kāhuna* have a prayer: "Let that which is unknown become known." This is an excellent prayer to hold in our minds as we begin to explore the Huna way.

Above all, it is important to remember that Huna is a philosophy of everyday life. If you took away the rituals, you would find universal principles of metaphysics, which is one reason I love it so much. Those same fourteen principles, the ones I have taught for many years, are as follows:

1. You create your own reality . . . every part of it. You create it through your own beliefs, expectations, attitudes, desires, fears, judgments, interpretations, feelings, and especially persistent thoughts.

2. You get what you concentrate on.

3. You are responsible for your own experience.

4. Thoughts will telepathically attract their equivalents:

   a) Positive thoughts attract positive people and events.

   b) Negative thoughts attract negative people and events.

5. Life presents to you whatever your thoughts are.

6. As you change your mind, you change your experience.

7. You are unlimited. There are no boundaries. God is infinite and unlimited; therefore, everything that is, is unlimited. Anything is possible. All you have to do is believe it.

8. The present is the fruit of the past and the seed of the future.

9. The world is what you think it is. You can change your world by changing your thoughts.

10. Energy flows wherever your attention goes.

11. Nothing ever happens to you without you calling for it, or without your participation.

12. All power comes from within.

13. You create exactly whatever your vibe is.

14. Think what you want because you are going to get what you think whether you want it or not.

Within this system, the most challenging aspect is this: Your unconscious thoughts as well as your conscious ones are producing results. That is exactly why you get weird results in your life that you didn't believe you wanted or needed. How can you change your unconscious, sabotaging thoughts when you don't even know what they are and when, by their nature, unconscious thoughts are hidden?

The greatest gift you can offer the world, yourself, and your children is a clear consciousness, free of distracting or sabotaging thoughts. In doing the transformational work of the *kahuna* way, you are locating sabotaging and negative thoughts, weeding them out, and literally creating a clearer consciousness to bring to the world. In trainings I offer, I teach people many different ways to process their own minds and discover these unconscious thoughts.

Hypnosis is one way, for it can help bring forth what exists just below the surface. But the easiest and quickest way to uncover unconscious thoughts is to do breathwork with a trained breathworker. In breathwork we learn ways to explore our unconscious thoughts and feelings through a process of following our breath.

One of the goals of Renewal Breathwork, one of the systems I teach, is to make the unconscious conscious so that we can see our thoughts, become conscious of what they are producing in our lives, and then have the choice to change them. A well-trained breathworker can help us identify even preverbal thoughts that trace back to our births and even the womb. Once we remove negative unconscious material from our minds, our whole lives can change.

At the core of the *kahuna* way is remembering to always think and speak positively. In *Fundamentals of Hawaiian Mysticism* (2000), Charlotte Berney tells us that approximately 80 percent of all unenlightened people's dialogue is negative. She adds that according to many Hawaiian *kāhuna*, if too much negativity accumulates in the Lower Self, it will unload the negativity by means of an accident or illness. As I write this, I am in Australia where aboriginal teachers express a similar belief: "Life is a dream and we dream our lives into being." And in the Bible: "As he thinketh in his heart, so is he" (Proverbs 23:7).

Given this perspective, all forms of blame are off track. I have said this in all of my books, but before I can go on to explain the deeper secrets of Huna, it is essential that you integrate the above and accept that thoughts create results. Without this complete understanding, you are nowhere. Does this, or any other system you might be following, really work for you? This system of recognizing the impact of our thoughts on our own and other people's lives always works. It teaches not only that whatever you think is what you get, but also that whatever you say is what you get. If you say, "My thoughts do not produce results," then you will get that result—nothing. There is no way around this, and why would you want there to be? After all, it works. You can create whatever you want and you can *uncreate* what you don't want.

In the old days these secrets were carefully guarded, held to be the exclusive property of the masters. Now we all need to become students of Huna and masters of our lives. *Now* is the moment of power.

Unique Principles Found in Huna Philosophy

What is unique about the Huna philosophy, making it even more effective than many other systems, are three important elements that it embodies:

1. A form of consciousness, called *no'ono'o*

2. A form of force, called *mana*

3. A form of substance, called *aka*

Brad Steiger (1997) explains that it is the consciousness *(no'ono'o)* that brings magic into being, the force *(mana)* that sustains it, and the substance *(aka)* through which the force can act. To make use of these three elements, however, requires that our lives be harmonious and whole.

The *kāhuna* acknowledge three selves in every person: Higher, Middle, and Lower. The Lower Self is similar to what today we call the unconscious mind; the Middle Self compares to what we call the conscious mind; the Higher Self corresponds to what we call the superconscious mind, or the part of the self that is capable of being in touch with the spirit.

Charlotte Berney (2000) observed that when these three selves perform their proper functions and interact with one another in a balanced, harmonious way, that person creates whatever is desired in life. The practice of Huna is one of bringing these selves into a working harmony for the purpose of having the life we desire.

Before putting all this together to demonstrate how to work the magic, I want to tell a story of a *kahuna* who exemplified perfect harmony between his three selves. He showed me the power of the full union of his three selves working as a team through the guidance of his Higher Self.

This story is about a *kahuna* named Al. I asked him to open my summer event in Kaua'i. Five hundred students, including my own mother, from all over the world would be in attendance. I was anxious for everyone to meet Al, but I had no idea what he was going to do. After we'd all gathered, he asked everyone to go outside and remove their shoes, telling them that what I was teaching was so holy that we must treat the conference room like a temple.

He did some chanting outside and put a flower lei on me and my mother. We also put one on him. When everyone was seated and very still, he got up on the stage and . . . said nothing. Suddenly he began to cry, and avalanches of love began to pour out of him. Within seconds, the whole room was crying, all five hundred of them! He never said a word. Not a single word. Now *that* was real power. My definition of true power is love, safety, and certainty, and in that moment he clearly demonstrated all three.

The next year I invited him again to open my summer event. He came to my room a half-hour early and lay down on the couch in my living room, covering himself completely with a gold cloth. After he had meditated, I begged him to sing a few chants to the group. He did not promise. Soon after, we went to meet the group together. I prepared a seat for him next to mine.

I was a bit worried about this event, as there was one man in the group who was very angry. I was afraid he would be a problem in the training. I hadn't mentioned this to Al.

Al sang one chant for us to begin the session. Then he called up the very man I was worried about and had him sit in my chair. He wrapped the gold cloth, soaked with his energy, around the man and put a crown on his head. The man immediately softened, as if his anger had drained away. He caused no trouble during the training. I was astonished by the way Al had read my mind so perfectly. He was aware of the situation and took care of it way ahead of time. This is what the *kāhuna* are like.

These three selves are also called three spirits in the Huna philosophy:

The **Lower Self** is called the "**Unihipili**" (pronounced "oo-nee-hee-pill-ee"):

1. It is like a computer in that it simply follows orders.

2. It is comparable to a servant.

3. It maintains the integrity of the body and oversees its operation.

4. It can remember but has only elementary reasoning power . . . somewhat comparable to the reasoning capacity of an animal.

5. It accepts and responds to suggestion.

6. Also called the "Basic Self," it is the mind that never sleeps.

7. Its consciousness is like that of a child.

8. Because it follows orders, it is important to develop a loving relationship with it, according to Serge King (1983).

9. It must be freed of all complexes of guilt or sin so that it will do its part happily whenever it is asked to send our prayers.

10. It must be told by the Middle Self that it is forgiven, cleansed, and greatly loved. Only when freed in

this way can it express love. Where there is no love, there is no energy to make prayer work. It will be ineffective.

11. Communication and contact with the Higher Self is impossible when the Lower Self is in opposition to the Middle Self.

12. Alone, it has no capacity for discernment and no discretion. For that reason, it requires guidance, love, caring, and concern. Explain to your Unihipili that this new system is preferable to others already programmed, such as old rituals and ceremonies and especially those based in religion.

The **Middle Self** is called the "**Uhane**" (pronounced "oo-hah-nay"):

1. It has the power to use the will and uses inductive reasoning, the highest known form of reason.

2. It has the task of undertaking to train the Lower Self.

3. It focuses on physical reality, analyzes it, integrates it, then forms beliefs, attitudes, and opinions about it.

4. It handles creative imagination.

5. It is the mind that talks.

6. It uses logic and makes decisions.

7. It functions only during waking hours.

8. It governs the intellect.

9. It vibrates at a higher frequency level and is more refined than the Unihipili.

10. Its role is to be the processor and to express concern to the Lower Self, the computer. It should be the Lower Self's leader and guide.

The **Higher Self** is called the **"Aumakua"** (pronounced "ow-mah-koo-ah"):

1. It is like an older, parental, trustworthy spirit, composed of masculine and feminine polarities.

2. It is called Father-Mother-God, your personal connection to the Higher Source, according to Charlotte Berney (2000).

3. It is the one that functions, along with your spirit guides and angels, to help you through life.

4. It is the source of insight and inspiration.

5. It is like a transformer between you and the cosmos.

6. It does not tell you what you should do, only what you can do. With it you have access to the knowledge of what to do to achieve a particular end and how to do it. (This knowledge may come through dreams, visions, inspirations, hunches, etc.)

7. Contact with it increases creativity and the ability to give of ourselves.

8. While it is part of us, it functions like a guardian angel, the father within, the personal savior.

9. To contact it, the Unihipili must deliver our prayers.

10. Unless it has vital force *(mana)* to work with conjointly, it cannot perform greatly and swiftly to help us on the dense physical level.

11. Unless vital force *(mana)* is sent with the prayer delivered by the Unihipili, nothing happens (Long 1955).

12. It has an incredible amount of power, a power sufficient to heal.

13. It has a very high frequency of vibration.

The practice of Huna brings these three selves— Unihipili, Uhane, and Aumakua—into a working harmony through frequent dialogue between them. If one self is consistently ignored, problems can occur. How does one accumulate the *mana* necessary for the system to work? For the *kahuna* the answer to this question is to breathe heavily. Stronger breathing is the first step in creating magic.

The conduit through which the vital force travels is an invisible cord called *aka*. *Aka* is a luminous extension away from the body. All things, including thoughts, possess a shadowy body, a sticky elastic substance, which some will know by the term "ectoplasm."

In breathwork, the Divine Breath (the vital energy) is sent to the subconscious where it is either stored or utilized, depending on the need of the moment. If healing or treatment is needed, then the conscious mind sends the request to the unconscious which, in turn, collects the energy with all the needed ingredients such as feelings in the memory banks, and joins forces with the conscious and the superconscious, who have access to all forces of the cosmos. The return flow of energy ushers in the answer, or result, to the prayer or request.

The Secrets of Effective Prayer

Because prayer is such an important part of following the *kahuna* way, it is important to know the secret for making it work. This is the key to manifesting results. One might say that the reason most prayers do not work is that they contain sabotaging thoughts, usually in the form of unconscious material that prevents the prayer from working. The unconscious, in that respect, is not cooperating with the higher consciousness. Furthermore, it is necessary to incorporate a breath technique during prayer, as this is key for creating exact desired results.

Effective prayer is connected to the abundance and free flow of *mana*. Remember that *mana* is the life force, the means by which the mind affects matter. It manifests as a flow or current, streaming in from another universe. Spiritual practices such as chanting can generate tremendous *mana*. Expressing appreciation during prayer also helps to raise *mana*.

Mana is universal divine spiritual power. It is stored in the body and manifests as what most of us recognize as vigor. It is always the goal of the *kahuna* to acquire and guard personal *mana*.

We can learn to direct *mana* to flow outward for the purpose of healing, achieving goals, and completing projects. The *kāhuna* say that the amount of *mana* we have in our command will determine our success and luck, or lack thereof. Blocks to *mana* are anger, resentment, guilt, anxiety, and negativity.

Mana originates in the supernatural realm but is a power possessed by all humans. It is an inherent quality in leadership. All high-impact personalities, that is, people with great personal magnetism and charisma, owe their power to the *mana* they possess. It is due to their *mana* that we see the power, genius, and inspiration of great kings.

To manifest goals, our Higher Self needs a sufficient supply of *mana*. The most effective way to gather *mana* is through deep breathing. Employing *mana* generators, such as crystals and pyramids, can help this process. *Mana* can also be absorbed from the environment by spending time around trees, hiking, and walking near the ocean. Your individual *mana* can extend beyond your physical body so that objects you own or handle can be invested with your spiritual power.

Mana originates in the supernatural realm but is a power possessed by all humans.

A belief in the power of prayer permeated the everyday lives of the early Hawaiians. Prayer was the most essential practice in their tradition. It is, in effect, the means by which Huna methods are accomplished.

The First Step Before Prayer is to Accumulate Extra *Mana*

Deep breathing practices help to clear the mind of all distractions. Here's how it works (adapted from Long 1955). (You may want to find a place to do this exercise where you will not be disturbed for at least twenty minutes.)

1. Empty your lungs as much as possible by exhaling forcefully, using the pressure of your chest muscles.

2. Breathe in slowly through your nose until your lungs are completely full.

3. Tightly purse your lips as if to whistle.

4. Slowly blow out the air.

5. Exhale forcefully.

6. Repeat all these steps several times.

The Ferson Method

The Ferson Method, named after Eugene Ferson, one of the first Europeans to be initiated into the Huna tradition during the nineteenth century, is another *mana*-generating exercise. It is as follows:

1. Stand with feet wide apart and arms extended level with your shoulders, palms angling slightly upward.

2. Hold this position and say out loud: "The universal life force is flowing into me now. I feel it."

3. Repeat four times, pausing twenty seconds between each repetition.

Formula for Prayer Action

The following formula is adapted from Max Freedom Long's *The Secret Science behind Miracles* (1948).

1. State the intention of your prayer clearly.

2. Gather abundant *mana.*

3. Send this *mana* to the Higher Self.

The Higher Self will use the vital force you draw in to formulate the answer to your prayer. The Higher Self has the ability to change the future and will bring about the desired condition. Remember, intention and *mana* work closely together to produce the result.

When the *mana* charge has been accumulated, hold the commanded desire in mind so that the Lower Self contacts the Higher Self by activating the *aka* thread of connection. Then call up the mental image of the desired condition and say, "I ask that this condition of (name or describe it) be made into reality in my future."

It is interesting to note that when the Christians came to the islands, the *kāhuna* were shocked by their practice of going to church to pray without breathing life into their prayers. Because of this, the Christians were called *"haole,"* which means "without breath." It was noted that the *haole* did not produce magic.

A clear path to the Higher Self enables the flow of *mana* to travel up the *aka* thread. You may recall that contact with the superconscious, or Higher Self, can only be accomplished by the Lower Self acting under orders from the Middle Self. The Lower Self is connected to the Higher Self by the *aka* thread. When the conscious mind and the unconscious mind are in agreement, the superconscious mind can take over. The problem for most people is that the unconscious mind has too many blocks that prevent this agreement; these blocks must be removed before the prayer can be fulfilled.

Understanding Blocks Between the Lower and Higher Self

If the Lower Self does something of which it is ashamed, it will try to avoid the Higher Self. Guilt and fear may collide, and the Lower Self will stubbornly refuse to make contact with the Higher Self. When that condition exists, preventing the proper manifestation of desires, one may seek out a *kahuna* for help. The *kahuna* will wonder why the person was unable to solve his or her own problems, as the Higher Self is capable of anything. Thus, the first thing the *kahuna* will do is look for a "complex."

A well-trained breathworker will do the same thing, that is, uncover the hidden agenda or sabotaging block. The cause of the block may prove to be anything from a sin imposed by the church, such as missing Confession or eating meat on Friday, to an actual physical, emotional, or spiritual injury inflicted upon another person.

If the person with the block has actually hurt another person, he or she must immediately seek forgiveness. In *Kahuna Magic* (1997), Brad Steiger suggests that neglecting forgiveness puts one in danger of "slamming the door" between the Lower Self and the Higher Self.

In order to remove the complex, and thus enable communication between the Lower and Higher Self, allowing prayers to work, a logical appeal must be made to the conscious self. A physical stimulus, such as sprinkling water or burning incense, may need to accompany the appeal.

The Higher Self must receive a clear, unwavering picture of whatever is desired by the person praying. If the Higher Self picks up the ambiguities, ambivalence, or contradictions and fragmentation of a constantly changing image, it will become confused and produce erroneous results. Think about this: How often do you waver back and forth and then wonder why your prayers are not answered? How often do you put out ambiguous or ambivalent messages, such as, "I want a relationship but am afraid I will get hurt." Examine your statements carefully, and you will soon understand why it would be difficult, or even impossible, for the Higher Self to fulfill your request.

Praise and Criticism

Around the time I visited the first cave on Maui, I met a wonderful *kahuna* named Serge King. Much of his writing is about praise and criticism. In line with the aloha spirit, he emphasizes that praise reinforces the good and allows it to increase and grow. Criticism, on the other hand, reinforces the bad and often destroys relationships.

King says, "When you criticize yourself, your *Ku* (masculine generative power) feels under attack and tries to defend itself by clenching muscles, which causes stress and inhibits awareness, memory, and energy flow, making you weaker and more subject to illness and accident" (1990). He further states that self-appreciation relaxes these muscles, increasing energy, and strengthening you.

He offers another important message: "When you criticize another, your *Ku* takes it personally and your body gets tense. When you praise another, your *Ku* says thank you and your body relaxes."

The most valuable lesson I learned from him is that love increases as judgment decreases.

Example of Prayer for Relationship

Beloved Divine Mother, Babaji, Ammachi, Kahuna, Divine Mother over all holy spirits, all the angels and all good forces necessary: I come before you this day and pray with all my heart and soul and mind to request humbly that I now receive into my life the mate to whom my love belongs, the mate of my being.

Bring forth anything that I have not looked at in myself that would prevent me from receiving this now. Bring it all forward and let me work on it now. I call forth all my unfinished business so that I may finish it, so I will be ready to meet the mate of my being.

I ask for this divine dispensation in the name of Christ, and I accept this as done, as is thy will.

My beloved unconscious mind, I hereby ask and command that you take this thought from prayer with all my mana, the vital force necessary to demonstrate this prayer to God, the source of our being. (Breathe three deep breaths.)

Beloved presence of God, Assembled Masters of God, let the rain of blessing fall.

Thank you.

Amen.

Best to do for thirty days.

Example of Prayer for Money

The following excerpt is reproduced from Joshua D. Stone's *Hidden Mysteries* (1997):

> *I hereby ask and humbly pray with all my heart and soul and mind for Divine Abundance made manifest through personal fortune and success.*
>
> *I am willing to move beyond fear in order to fulfill God's Plan on Earth and Beyond.*
>
> *I personally pledge to open myself to financial wealth in order to fulfill my group and individual service commitments.*
>
> *In God's name, I accept my divine heritage Right Now and thank thee for the timely answer to this prayer.*
>
> *God's Will be Done.*
>
> *Amen.*
>
> Repeat this prayer out loud three times.

Beloved Prescence of God: *Oh, my beloved Unconscious mind, I hereby ask and lovingly command that you take this thought form prayer to God, along with the* mana *and vital force needed and necessary to manifest and demonstrate this prayer. Amen.*

Breathe the prayer to God four times.

Each time, upon completing the prayer, empty your lungs, breathe in and fill your lungs, then purse your lips and exhale, holding an image in your mind that your breath is carrying your message to God, whatever your understanding of God may be . . .

Wait ten to fifteen seconds.

Say, "Lord, let the rain of blessings fall."

Amen.

Feel the energy coming from God back to you. You might experience this as a flowing of energy or a tingling sensation anywhere in your body. Soak it in.

Sing peacefully and with devotion: Om Om Om.

An Auspicious Meeting and Celebration

When I met my first *kahuna* teacher, the great Morrnah Simeona, it was a big surprise. I'd been invited to a luncheon at a beach home in Honolulu. I had not been told that she, or any other *kahuna* for that matter, would be there. Shortly after my boyfriend, organizer, and I arrived, Morrnah, a strong-looking Native Hawaiian woman, entered the living room. I spontaneously burst into tears at the sight of her. I did not know a thing about the *kahuna* at the time, so I wondered how anyone could have had such a powerful affect on me.

My hosts seated me next to Morrnah. Suddenly, my head went down onto the empty plate in front of me and I could not raise it up. Tears flowed again. I turned my head slightly and out of the corner of my eye I looked at Morrnah: "Would you mind telling me what you're doing?"

"Oh," she said, "just a little interplanetary crystal cleansing."

Those were her first words to me. Then my boyfriend had his head in his plate, just like me, and my organizer had to leave the table and lie down. Moments later, the hostess came in and quipped, "Where's the quiche?"

I suggested (still with my head down) that she look on the kitchen floor—maybe the chef was down, too. Though I was partly joking, the hostess turned, went into the kitchen, and discovered that the chef, indeed, was on the floor. I cannot remember what happened after that. All I know is that at that moment, I had met my Hawaiian teacher.

At the time, I was living on the O'ahu coast in a lovely

home that hung over a cliff overlooking the ocean. It seemed like such a special place. The swimming pool, for example, was half outside and half inside the living room. I could swim in and out of the house! The pool hung over the cliff that offered a stunning view of the ocean. The only trouble was that my boyfriend could never sleep. He kept having dreams of flying spears. After hearing this several times, I called Morrnah and told her we needed to have the house cleansed.

I drove to Honolulu and picked her up in my sports car. As we drove back out to my house, I kept thinking about how surreal it was to be racing along in my car with a *kahuna* sitting beside me. At some point, Morrnah shouted, "What is in the northeast corner of your house?"

"I don't know, Morrnah. That's why I'm bringing you out!"

When we arrived at the house, she went straight to the northeast corner, which in fact was the pool. She immediately became very upset, pointing to the huge lava rock inside the pool. It had been placed there for decoration and for swimmers to dive from. She told me the that rock should have never been removed from the Big Island.

"Well," I said. "I don't know what to do about that. It came with the house."

I was new to the islands and so had not yet learned about the curses that befell people who took volcanic rocks from the Big Island. Apparently so much tragedy happens to people that take even little rocks that hundreds are sent back to the Park Service every week.

Morrnah told me she would meditate and see if anything could be done. I went upstairs and peered over the railing at her. I actually saw her transfiguring into a man! I found out later that *kahuna* can do that, so it was not just my imagination.

Twenty minutes later she said she would call me in a few days with the verdict but that it did not look good. In three days she called and told me I had to move out. She said that the placement of the rock was not the only error that had been made. The gods were also angry because the house had been built on a Hawaiian fish hatchery. And to make matters worse, it was built with funds stolen from the local sea aquarium. Morrnah explained that the combination of the three things made it impossible to clear the energy.

We moved out. I later heard that people who tried to live in that beautiful place were never able to make their relationships work.

I learned quickly that you don't mess around in Hawai'i. There are rules. The life of the land is preserved in righteousness. In old Hawai'i, behavior that offended a god or committed a *kapu* (something forbidden) could throw the individual or a whole community into imbalance.

Charlotte Berney notes that for the individual, imbalance could mean illness, bad luck, or some form of unhappiness that would shadow the person until balance could be restored. For the community, imbalance could mean failed crops or the coming of a natural disaster (2000).

Today, as in old Hawai'i, a healthy life is one that maintains balance between the material and spiritual realms. For the ancient ones there was never any separation between these realms.

What are you doing that might be out of integrity? Scrutinize yourself.

'*Ohana* Consciousness

The family, family clan, or extended family is called the '*ohana*. Again, "*ha*" means breath and so an '*ohana* was a family that did conscious breathing together. The use of breath was at the core of the family's spiritual practice.

In old Hawai'i, the family's consciousness of their origin was a deeply felt and unifying force. When family members died, they remained very much a part of the '*ohana*, though they were now in spirit form (Pukui, Hertig, and Lee 1972). One's relatives were both earthly and in spirit. Both were looked to for advice, instruction, and emotional support. Thus, communication with the supernatural was a normal part of everyday life.

People not related by a bloodline could also be admitted to the 'ohana status. Today 'ohana can include any group of people of like mind and purpose. Hence, with Morrnah's permission, I considered those who had taken my Loving Relationships Training as members of the 'ohana. This seemed appropriate since we would all lie down and breathe together.

The concept of 'ohana is wonderful because it indicates a sense of unity, shared involvement, and shared responsibility. It is about interdependence and mutual help. There is emotional support, solidarity, and cohesiveness. Who wouldn't want to be part of the 'ohana? The term also implies generosity, friendliness, patience, and productivity. This is why I try to create communities of like spirits wherever I go.

In Hawai'i, elders were always respected for their wisdom and experience. They had a very important role in guiding the children. It was believed that children should

> The concept of 'ohana is wonderful because it indicates a sense of unity, shared involvement, and shared responsibility. It is about interdependence and mutual help.

learn from them while they were still alive. The elders planted seeds in the hearts and minds of the children.

Sibling cooperation was also an important part of the *'ohana.* Everyone helped each other. Spiritual concerns pervaded much of the interaction between the people. The main rule was never to hurt another. It was believed that when you hurt someone, you hurt and disrupt the harmonious relationship with the "powers that be," that is, the powers that extended into the spiritual realms. Therefore, you must also ask forgiveness from them. Holding grudges not only caused one to be cut off from the family, but it also threatened an individual's relationship with the spiritual forces in ways that could jeopardize the individual or other innocent family members (Shook 1986).

Are you disrupting your relationship with the powers that be because you refuse to forgive, refuse to stop fighting and hurting, or refuse to cooperate?

Touching the Heart of the Islands

Morrnah told me that each island is a chakra and that Maui is the heart chakra.

I decided that the best way for me to experience this as deeply as I could would be to hike through the Haleakalā Crater. To do this, I had to get

Morrnah told me that each island is a chakra and that Maui is the heart chakra.

permission from the park rangers far in advance. Only a few people are allowed into the crater at a time because it is an environmentally fragile area.

I was shocked to learn that it is impossible to cross the crater in one day—that's how big it is. A one-night stay in a cabin deep inside the crater is a must. I talked my boyfriend, my Hawai'i organizer, and Len, the founder of rebirthing, into going with me. I did not particularly plan to go in with three men, but that is how it turned out.

Entering the crater and going down inside it is what it must be like to land on the moon. (I've been told that the astronauts did some of their training for the moon shot there.) Huge multicolored cinder cones, all of them very beautiful, are at every turn. The only species of plant that grows in the crater is the silversword. The silversword is on the endangered species list, one of the reasons the trail is so carefully protected. The plant grows only in this area at elevations between 6,800 and 9,800 feet. It is said that the silversword flowers only once, at the end of its fifteen- to fifty-year lifecycle.

It is so quiet in the crater that once you go into a deep

meditation, you stay in it. At night it was quite cold, even inside the cabin. What stands out most from that experience is the last day of our excursion, when we arrived at the other side of the crater and realized we had to hike up and out again.

At the top of the other side of the crater is a steep descending path that is quite rough on the shins. The path leads to an amazing plush rain forest. From there you can head down alongside seven sacred pools, each one representing a chakra and falling into the next one, all the way to the ocean. Wild orchids drip from their stalks everywhere. It is simply impossible to imagine such beauty. It is like the Garden of Eden.

At the end of the hike, I walked off and ended up near another pool. While staring down at that pool, a little Hawaiian boy, four or five years old, approached me. He said that if I dove into that pool and swam underwater, I would come up into a cave where the queen used to cool herself! He said there was a natural throne in there. He also said the cave would be dark and the water very cold, but if I waited the whole space would magically light up.

I was astonished by the boy's knowledge and command of the language. I knew he was telling the truth. To this day I don't know who he really was—maybe my guru appearing to me in the form of a child?

My friends thought I was crazy as they watched me

dive into the pool. It was freezing cold and I had to swim underwater for quite a while. Finally I came up into the cave. When I got there it was very dark, as the boy had said.

I also found the natural throne, formed by lava that had somehow cooled in mid-air over the pool I was swimming in. I climbed up the throne and sat there trying to imagine what it was like to be a Hawaiian queen. I started seeing apparitions such as an Egyptian queen lying next to me. For some reason this did not frighten me. I wondered whether there could be a connection between the *kāhuna* and Egyptians.

As I sat, I began to feel a tremble up and down my spine. It was my first real *kundalini* experience. Needless to say I did not want to leave. But after some time my friends began shouting for me to come out.

Many days later I told Morrnah about the little boy, the pool, and the cave. Morrnah looked at me oddly. "How did you get out of there alive?"

I was so surprised by her question I almost said, "Oh, but I'm a student of physical immortality. It was no problem for me." However, this did not seem appropriate.

I would often become speechless in Morrnah's presence and later have lapses of memory about what had happened when we were together. Only after we'd parted and gone our separate ways that day did I remember that I hadn't asked her why she said that about the cave.

Morrnah's *Ho'oponopono* Teachings

The greatest thing Morrnah taught me was how to do a prayer called *ho'oponopono*. We had decided for her to do a three-day course in my Seattle home for my friends on the mainland. I flew Morrnah and my mother over for the event.

Ho'oponopono is a long prayer (which includes special breathing) to correct mistakes and set relationships aright. It works to clear psychic attachments to people, places, and things. It is incredibly effective. I try to do it almost every day as one of my main spiritual practices.

At the end of Morrnah's three-day course, I received a book containing the prayer after promising to never give the book away. It must be directly handed down from a *kahuna* so that the power is never diluted. The book is only for those who have taken the course; however, I was told that I could do the prayer and rituals as a gift for other people. I do this often, usually inviting anyone around me to participate in my Hawaiian prayers.

Recently, I have studied many books and found versions of *ho'oponopono* that can be done without the course. In one excellent source, *Ho'oponopono: Contemporary Uses of a Hawaiian Problem-Solving Process* (1986), the author states: *"Ho'oponopono* may well be one of the soundest methods to restore and maintain good family relationships that any society has ever devised."

Now that is quite a claim! But having experienced the process many times myself, I can vouch for its validity. Holding a master's degree in family sociology, I have studied conflict resolution extensively but have never found anything nearly as powerful as *ho'oponopono*.

> "Ho'oponopono may well be one of the soundest methods to restore and maintain good family relationships that any society has ever devised"
> —E. Victoria Shook

Imagine having a technique available to you that can clear any family problems or disputes. Who wouldn't want a system for maintaining harmonious relationships and resolving conflict?

Purpose and Use of *Ho'oponopono*

H*o'oponopono* is a major Hawaiian gift. The name itself means "setting it right." Here are some of the ways it can benefit us:

1. It is a system for maintaining good relationships not only among family, friends, and colleagues but also with the supernatural powers.

2. It is a problem-solving process.

3. It can release the negative effects of past and present actions in our lives by spiritually, mentally, and physically cleansing through the processes of repentance, forgiveness, and transmutation.

4. It is a process for righting errors and creating balance.

5. It is a process for making right any stressful relationship or situation in life. All are set free from tensions created in these relationships.

6. It is a process for looking at ourselves to see how we contributed to the problem.

7. It is getting the family together to find out what is wrong—maybe to find out why someone is sick or to find the real cause of a quarrel.

8. It is a very sophisticated method of conflict resolution.

9. It embraces spiritual truths, thus lending dignity to the process of conflict resolution.

10. It is a problem-solving system that includes the following seven processes:

- **Prayer**—asking for guidance and support from a higher power

- **Statement of the problem**—articulating the problem so that all involved hear it

- **Discussion**—each person involved telling their side of the issue

- **Confession of wrongdoing**—persons who've caused the damage or difficult feelings taking responsibility for what has happened

- **Restitution**—an arrangement for bringing balance and understanding to all concerned, often in the form of a contract of action for righting a wrong

- **Forgiveness**—people who've been injured releasing the bonds between themselves and the perpetrator

- **Release**—reciting a prayer or performing a ritual to release all parties from present bonds created by the offending actions

How *Ho'oponopono* Works with the Invisible Cords

In the *kahuna* tradition the wrong-doer and the wronged are linked together by the transgression itself and by the chain of after-effects that it entails. The *kāhuna's* name for the transgression, fault, or error is *"hala."* We can imagine the *hala* as an invisible cord binding the offender to his deed and to his victim. As long as the victim holds onto this cord, he or she is bound to the perpetrator. And so it is that perpetrator and victim are held in subjugation to one another. The *kāhuna* knew that this would remain a relationship of negative entanglement until both victim and perpetrator were released through forgiveness.

The *hala* of an offense, large or small, can easily become a tangled web in which every member is snarled. Just as in a spider's intricately woven web, any disturbance in any part of it will tug at all other parts.

In the kahuna tradition the wrong-doer and the wronged are linked together by the transgression itself and by the chain of after-effects that it entails. The kahuna's name for the transgression, fault, or error is *"hala."*

When addressed through the *ho'oponopono* process, the *hala* is released through forgiveness. For example, as you loosen your brother from his trespasses, you release yourself from your own bond with him and from that trespass he has committed. As you forgive, you are also forgiven. That process is called "*kala,*" which literally means "to release, untie, unbind." To complete the liberation of victim and perpetrator from these bonds, and dissolve the web that may envelop others around them, each must release himself as well as the other from the deed. Both must let go of the cord (Pukui, Hertig, and Lee 1972).

Accomplishing this is like saying: "I unbind you from the fault, and thus may I be unbound from it." It is amazing to be part of such a process. It should be noted that this is very different from "forgiving and forgetting." In that system, what is forgotten could actually just be repressed, only to return in some other, usually unpredictable form. *Kala* strips away all painful after-effects of the repressed material that might otherwise be bound in the more simplistic forgiving and forgetting system so many of us have learned in our lives.

Those who choose to participate in the *'ohana* are charged with the duty of restoring balance and harmony through self-scrutiny, admitting wrongdoings, asking for forgiveness from their victims, and then making restitution. In *ho'oponopono* everyone searches their heart for hard feel-

> For the *kahuna*, forgiveness is the process of making the decision that whatever happened in the past is no longer important. For that reason, to claim you have forgiven when you actually have not is a great error, violating a deeper truth.

ings—anger, resentment, fear—against one another. Before God, and with His help, they forgive and are forgiven. It is in this way that they remove every grudge, peeve, or resentment among them (Shook 1986). For the *kahuna*, forgiveness is the process of making the decision that whatever happened in the past is no longer important. For that reason, to claim you have forgiven when you actually have not is a great error, violating a deeper truth. It is like dropping a huge rock in your own bowl of light.

Attitudes Required for *Ho'oponopono*

If the process is to be given a chance to work, everyone involved must bring themselves to the moment of healing with a mind of openness and positivity. This attitude is characterized as follows:

1. There must be the belief that problems can be definitely resolved if approached properly.

2. It must be approached with a true intention to correct wrongs.

3. The confession of error must be full and honest.

4. Prayers and forgiving and freeing must come from the heart (Pukui, Hertig, and Lee 1972).

5. There must be nothing withheld.

6. There must be full awareness that neither a crying fit nor a shouting match will solve the problem.

7. Everyone talks openly about their feelings and resentments, but not simply for cathartic purposes. The safety valve of discussion is used as a preventive measure so that minor disputes do not lead to major grievances.

8. "Talking things out" is not enough. Something constructive must be done about the cause of the grudge.

9. Participating in this process requires maturity.

10. Total truth is required without intentional omission or slanting of facts.

11. All essential material must be told, no matter how painful this may be.

12. Telling must never be vindictive or delivered with a desire to hurt (Pukui, Hertig, and Lee 1972).

13. When a person comes to you and asks for your forgiveness, you cannot turn your back on them. You have to forgive fully and completely.

14. The person asking for forgiveness must remain humble throughout. A lying apology is a lie to the Higher Self and God. Offending one is offending all. Making peace with one is making peace with all (Pukui, Hertig, and Lee 1972).

Conducting the Council

H*oʻoponopono* may be conducted by an elder who is knowledgeable about the process. Sometimes this is a *kahuna*, sometimes not. Preferably, everyone is seated on the floor in a circle. The meeting begins with all participants joining hands and bowing their heads. The person conducting the meeting recites an opening prayer, or *pule*. Here is an example of one such prayer:

Dear Heavenly Father/Mother, we thank thee for this opportunity to get together. Give us the strength and wisdom and understanding to be able to lay the problems out and identify what the problems are. Give us the understanding and know-how to be able to discuss things in a way that makes for understanding. Give us the opportunity so that as one is talking the others will sit quietly and listen with an open ear. And dear Lord, after we have identified it all, may we be able to open our hearts to one another to forgive each other so that we can carry on always. We are in thy holy name.
Amen.

In the case where a family member is sick, the *pule* (prayer or blessing) might be as follows:

Oh, Jehova, God, Creator of Heaven and Earth and his son, Jesus Christ. We ask for your help. To our Aumakua from east and west, north and south, from zenith of horizon and from upper strata to lower. Hearken. Come! We want to get your guidance and help so we can know what is wrong with (name).
God please provide the spiritual strength we need to work out this problem. Help us to help ourselves.
Amen. *

After the prayer, the following takes place:

1. The persons involved make statements about the obvious problem to be solved.

2. There is a discussion of the perpetrator and victim's conduct, followed by self-scrutiny, conducted with absolute truthfulness and sincerity.

3. Disruptive emotions are prevented by channeling discussions through the leader.

4. The leader questions all involved participants.

5. The perpetrator makes an honest confession to God.

6. Immediate restitution or an arrangement for restitution is made to the injured party.

7. There is an exchange of mutual forgiveness, thus releasing one another from all guilt, grudges, and tensions caused by the wrongdoing.

8. The leader may call breaks for periods of silence.

9. The leader offers a closing prayer.

---

* During the missionary years in Hawai'i, many Hawaiians adopted Christian thought. Today, when speaking to large numbers of Hawaiian people, these Christian concepts and terms are often used.

What It Might Look Like

The following is an example of a meeting conducted in the case of sibling disharmony caused by a child stealing from his brother. After saying the *pule,* the leader says to the wronged brother: "Remember, as you loosen your brother from his trespasses, you loosen yourself, too. As you forgive, you are forgiven." Then:

Leader: (to perpetrator) Who do you want to forgive you?

Perpetrator: God and my brother.

Leader: Are you ready to ask for this forgiveness?

Perpetrator: Yes.

Leader: Hear, God, that (name) is sorry. Please forgive him his trespasses. He is sorry for what he has done. (Recites prayer) Now we will make an arrangement for restitution. (Name), are you willing to take a small job to earn enough to pay back your brother? There must be a sacrifice.

Perpetrator: I am willing.

Everyone affected by the problem in some way is asked

The *ho'oponopono* is highly structured, with many built-in controls that assist the participants to release one another from their negative bond.

to share their feelings in a calm manner. They agree to listen to one another as they speak. They agree to avoid blame. If tempers flare, the leader calls for a break of silence or prayerful contemplation.

When the discussion is complete, there is a sincere confession of wrongdoing and the seeking of forgiveness. It is expected that forgiveness is given whenever it is requested. Failure to forgive can precipitate repercussions from the spiritual world and from group members (Shook 1986). The *ho'oponopono* is highly structured, with many built-in controls that assist the participants to release one another from their negative bond. There must be insistence that disagreeing family members refrain from directly addressing one another. They speak to the leader in all cases. There can be no acting out of intense feelings.

At the end of *ho'oponopono,* the resolved problem is declared closed, never to be brought up again. What a wonderful arrangement! How many people keep bringing up old hurts?

Ho'oponopono offers one of the best methods I know of, regardless of its cultural roots, for creating and maintaining good family relationships.

If you do not feel ready or capable to be the leader, maybe you can find someone else who will. At least you got things going. If you are unable to find someone, this is why it is good to take the course and have the book so it can be done properly and telepathically

Couples' Conflict Resolution the *Ho'oponopono* Way

In *Fundamentals of Hawaiian Mysticism* (2000), Charlotte Berney describes how *ho'oponopono* may be helpful in romantic relationships. The process is simple:

1. One person calls for the session to address a specific problem.

2. When the other person agrees, the couple decides on a time and place free of distractions.

3. The couple begins the session with a prayer, asking their Higher Selves, guides, angels, and guardians to be present; and their Lower Selves to fully cooperate.

4. The couple agrees ahead of time not to use angry voices but to speak calmly without interruption.

5. They agree not to say things that would hurt the other.

6. The person who called the session speaks for five minutes uninterrupted, stating the nature of the problem and why it needs to be examined and resolved.

7. The other person speaks for five minutes uninterrupted, stating their understanding of the problem.

8. Then, each person speaks in turn about how this problem made them feel and how they would prefer to feel.

9. Each speaks on how both have contributed to the problem.

10. Each speaks on how both could contribute to solving the problem.

11. Each states steps they could take to release the problem from their lives.

12. The person who called the session summarizes what has just been accomplished, reporting it as accurately as possible.

13. Both make a statement of commitment to the relationship and to living in harmony.

I was amazed to find this simple procedure in a book, since I had been teaching nearly this exact technique for many years. Had it just been obvious or logical to me? Had I channeled it? Or had I actually recalled the process from ancient times? Whatever the source, this process has always proved to be highly effective.

While *ho'oponopono* is usually done in small, private groups, Morrnah gave me permission to do it with larger groups. For example, whenever I teach a class on Maui, people come from all over the world. I love to take the whole class down to the foot of the Haleakala Crater. We do *ho'oponopono* outside, right there, which greatly increases the power of the teachings, as this is where the process is said to have originated.

The Power of *Ho'oponopono*

While reading the *ho'oponopono* prayer in the book I was given, I reached a part where the words are also given in

Hawaiian. I sat there staring at the page, wishing I could speak Hawaiian or that there was someone with me who could recite the prayer in Hawaiian, as it is so lovely. At that moment Auntie Pua and Auntie Maile came walking up the hill! I hadn't mentioned to them at all where I was going to be or what I would be doing that day.

I handed them the book. They proceeded to recite the following in the Hawaiian language, speaking it freely, like the hula, just as I had wished:

"I" AM THE "I"
OWAU NO KA "I"

"I" come forth from the void into light,
Pua mai au mai ka po iloko o ka malamalama,

"I" am the breath that nurtures life,
Owau no ka ha, ka mauli ola,

"I" am that emptiness, that hollowness beyond all
consciousness,
Owau no ka poho, ke ka'ele mawaho a'e o no ike apau,

The "I", the Id, the All.
Ka I, Ke Kino Iho, na Mea Apau.

"I" draw my bow of rainbows across the waters,
Ka a'e au i ku'u pi'o o na anuenue mawaho a'e o na kai a pau,

The continuum of minds with matters.
Ka ho'omaumau o na mana'o ame na mea a pau.

"I" am the incoming and outgoing of breath,
Owau no ka "Ho", a me ka "Ha,"

The invisible, untouchable breeze,
He huna ka makani nahenahe,

The undefinable atom of creation.
Ka "Hua" huna o Kumulipo.

"I" am the "I."
Owau no ka "I."

Later, I was doing *ho'oponopono* at a meeting in Paris, France, during a time when people were mad at the French for their nuclear testing in Fiji. There was a huge demonstration in Paris, protesting the testing. Nothing was moving in the city. Everything was closed down, including cabs, buses, and the underground subway. As we listened to the news and heard reports from friends, I was expecting to have to cancel my seminar.

But this was not to be. Breathworkers and students I had never met came on bicycles and parked them in the hotel lobby. Within a short period of time, the seminar room was packed. It was amazing.

I had everyone write down what they wanted to clear for the *ho'oponopono* prayers. There were several hundred French people in the room. After I finished the prayer, I told them to tear up the papers and give them to the assistants who would come around with two big bags. The audience was instructed not to drop even the tiniest piece of paper—everything must go into the bags.

After collecting all of the paper, both assistants came toward me, one on the left side of the room, one on the right . . . and—I will never forget this—they both tripped at exactly the same moment! Thousands of tiny scraps of paper flew all over the floor. Immediately, everyone was down on their hands and knees picking up all the paper. It was very funny, and yet it seemed appropriate because of what was going on in the country. Here was a whole room full of people, down on the floor, working together to correct their collective karma.

The *Kāhuna* and Healing

In ancient times, the *kāhuna* maintained a belief system that was simple and free from dogmas, in spite of influences brought in by many religions. Their way of life worked, and they did everything they could to sustain and hold what they knew in a sacred way. I have seen the magic of the *kahuna* way, have experienced it myself, and have been doing *hoʻoponopono* for many years. According to the *kāhuna*, all healing is the result of a natural communion with the God-Self, allowing this source of energy to flow freely in its original pattern.

Among their many lessons, the *kāhuna* teach that illness and distortion of any kind results from interference with the natural flow of the energy that comes from our source. Within their view of the world, all symptoms are a

Among their many lessons, the *kāhuna* teach that illness and distortion of any kind results from interference with the natural flow of the energy that comes from our source. Within their view of the world, all symptoms are a form of conversion reaction, that is, of an emotional, mental, or spiritual imbalance that has taken physical form.

form of conversion reaction, that is, of an emotional, mental, or spiritual imbalance that has taken physical form. It was interesting for me to discover how this same view of illness is found in other spiritual traditions and disciplines.

Recently, on my way back from Australia where I had been teaching, I landed in Hawai'i to teach another workshop. The next morning, I woke up shouting: "Something is terribly wrong in my family."

I immediately called home but could not get in touch with my mom. My niece, however, was able to tell me what was happening. Mom was very ill and had been taken to the hospital. Because she hadn't wanted me to worry, she hadn't told me what was going on. I tuned into what was happening with her and immediately knew she was dying.

I called Mom and was able to talk with her at the hospital. She said she was not ready for me to come home. She had not yet cleaned up her place properly—she didn't want to offend her Virgo daughter! Regardless, I scheduled the next flight home after my Hawai'i seminar that weekend. Even after making these arrangements, though, I did not feel comfortable. I could feel Mom starting to go out of her body, and I felt the pull. I was having symptoms similar to hers. I felt horrible and could not stay in my body. I knew I was going to get very sick if I didn't take some drastic action. But more than my own discomfort, I realized that what I was experiencing was even worse for Mom.

I contacted a friend and after some effort we located an old *kahuna* over on the Lahaina side of the island. My friend drove me to his place, all the while coaching me as I did breathwork. As we turned into the driveway, the *kahuna* came out of the house and shouted at me to hurry. Then he scurried back into the house. I scrambled from the car and made my way to the door. Inside the house, the *kahuna* had his hands on a patient who was seated in a chair in the middle of the room. There were chairs lined up all around the room where people were waiting to be treated.

"What has happened to you, sister?" he shouted at me, not missing a beat or taking his hands off his patient. I told him my situation. He told his assistants to heat up the rocks, which were in a canvas bag, in a microwave oven. Now that was a new one for me—modern technology serving ancient healing techniques. "These are not ordinary rocks," the *kahuna* explained. He had picked them up on the beach, being ever so selective and choosing each one separately.

As I waited for my turn, the *kahuna*'s assistant rubbed the hot bag of rocks up and down my body, explaining that it would help me get me back into my body. After half an hour, my turn came. The *kahuna* straightened me out so that I was able to get back to the seminar.

Much to my surprise, Auntie Pua and Auntie Maile came to my hotel room and talked to me as I got ready. Not only that, but they were both wearing red, perfectly matching my own red dress. I always marvel at how I have never had to call my *kahuna* friends to come.

My two friends escorted me to the seminar room and began chanting, staying with me most of the time to keep me in my body. To have a *kahuna* with me anywhere, anytime is pure bliss. But this was a very special time, with special needs that required extraordinary measures, not only for me but for my mom as well.

Though I did not request it, my *kahuna* friends stayed with me through the whole seminar. I also had network chiropractors in the room who helped me. The support was amazing. I got on a plane immediately after the seminar. After Mom saw me, she left her body, but then the medical team resuscitated her and she came back. This was such a blessing, as she had a lot of secrets to tell me. Then Mom died, beginning a huge process for me that went on for many years.

I was so happy that I had introduced Mom to all my healing "team." I felt it made her passing easier. In fact, my guru, Babaji, actually appeared to her in the hospital before she left, so I knew she was in good hands. She was ready to go and wanted to, so I had to let go.

Powerful Philosophies of Healing

The great skill of the *kahuna* healers stems from their reverence for life. They know the body cannot respond to any kind of treatment without first being healed, mentally and spiritually. They use the art of suggestion. This sometimes consists of transferring some of the *mana*, or vital force, from the universe to the person being healed. While lying on hands, they act like a conduit, transferring a flow of *mana* to the sick person. They know that if a physical stimulus such as hands is employed, along with mild suggestions for inner harmony and balance, the healing work is enhanced.

The *kāhuna* share their joy, knowing that joy is life-giving and expansive. It releases tension and acts like an invitation to the Higher Self to become a full partner in bringing about health. They know that joy-filled cooperation, along with the motto "God in Everything," is the best medicine for all ills.

Papa Kalua, like all *kāhuna*, taught that illness is not caused by bacteria, viruses, or carcinogenic agents, but by tension resulting from conflicts. Serge King (1983) points out that the *kāhuna* never said that germs don't exist, but only that they are byproducts of the disease rather than the cause. Even lack of necessary nutrients in a person is not thought to be caused by inadequate diet, but by certain types of thinking that result in imbalance. They would say it is not what goes into a man's mouth that defiles him, but what comes out of it.

The special magic of instant healing is accomplished by the *kāhuna* through the aid of the Higher Self. For example, in *Kahuna Magic* (1997), Brad Steiger discusses how Hawaiian healers were able to cure broken bones instantly. The Higher Self first dissolved the injured bone and other tissues into ectoplasm. Since ectoplasm is an etheric substance, it cannot be broken or injured. Then, molding the ectoplasm using the template of the normal leg there at hand, the ectoplasmic material was once again solidified. Obviously a very high flow of vital force had to be employed to accomplish all of this.

When a *kahuna* prayed to his own Higher Self, asking for its assistance to help a client, the prayer automatically went to the Higher Self of the client as well.

Emotional and spiritual pain or illness was also healed by the *kāhuna*, as we've already illustrated in the *ho'oponopono* discussions above. *Kāhuna* believed that complete healing of such "dis-eases" could only come with complete forgiveness of the whole family.

When people got very sick, especially if it involved

paralysis, they were taken to the ocean while it was still dark, placed in the water, and massaged as the sun came up. Facing the sun, the healers would chant and massage, using a form of massage called *lomilomi*. In three days, even a paralyzed person would walk again (King 1990)!

Opening the Blocks to Heal

I found the early *kahuna* interpretation of insanity very interesting. They felt it resulted when the conscious self, Uhane (Middle Self), was displaced and a new Uhane did not take over command of the body. This displacement of the Uhane could happen as the result of an accident, serious illness, curse, or shock. This left the resident unconscious, Unhipili (Lower Self), in charge of the person's life. Remember that alone the Unihipili has no capacity for discernment or discretion. It is like a leaf on the wind and therefore highly impressionable. For that reason, it counts on the Middle Self for guidance, love, caring, stability, and concern.

The *kāhuna* view the human physical body as an intensely energized thought form. It is as much an expression of the individual self as is a painting or sculpture. It is your creation, which is why it responds to your thoughts.

For healing to take place, the paths that the energies follow in our lives must be open. The "path," the "way," or the "light" are all symbolic terms used to describe the ways of connection between the Lower Self and the Higher Self. An example of blocking the path is this: If the Lower Self is convinced that the person is guilty of a wrong act, it feels shamed and refuses to communicate with the Higher Self. Since prayers, in any healing, must be communicated to the Higher Self through the Lower Self, nothing can happen until the Lower Self is cleared of its feelings of guilt or shame (Long 1948).

The first step in healing is for the person to reduce his guilt complexes to the minimum and free himself of dogmatic religious beliefs. In *The Secret Science behind Miracles* (1948), Long states that the *kāhuna* think in terms of the saying "Nothing gets hardening of the arteries as fast as religion." The *kāhuna* who maintained their original ways even after the missionary period in the islands felt that religious fixations were frequently the cause of guilt, and thus illness. The reason for this is that sin is always associated with intense guilt. And by its nature, guilt demands punishment. Dogmas that teach us that we are guilty or unworthy can block prayers of healing unless a clearing of those feelings is first performed.

One way to determine whether a blocking of this kind

exists is to look at the results following any healing. In breathwork, we say results are your guru. If you are not getting results from the work, you have to identify the sabotaging fixation you are holding onto. A well-trained breathworker, like a *kahuna* healer, knows how to do that and helps you breathe out the fixation or block so that you can open yourself to healing.

If a fixed sense of guilt is strong and stubborn, it will help greatly to do a daily good deed in a most impersonal way without expecting either thanks or a reward. In other words, a good deed accomplished that is completely free of any self-serving attitudes or expectations. According to Long (1955), this establishes in the Lower Self a deep feeling that good has been done to balance the former wrong of hurting another.

When you feel tingling or the sensation of your hair standing on its end, it is a sign that the Lower Self has received the message and is relieved of the feelings that would otherwise be preventing it from communicating with the Higher Self. Belief on the part of the Middle Self is not enough. Faith is necessary, and only when the Lower Self also believes is there genuine faith.

As discussed earlier, all healing is accomplished through communication between the Lower Self and the Higher Self. In making a prayer to the Higher Self, the thought forms of the prayer must be clear and direct, not mixed up with doubts and uncertainties. Most people send to the Higher Self a continuous jumble of unclear, conflicting, and double-messaged wishes and fears. For example, it is not enough to say, "I want a new relationship to come into my life." Rather, we need to state the kind of relationship we desire: "I want a loving and caring relationship in which we can both enjoy a sense of equality."

Specificity is key. If your prayer is this: "I have money problems and want to be free of them," think of all the ways it could be interpreted and then fulfilled. It could result in anything from winning the lottery, thereby allowing you to pay off your debts, to going to jail, where your money problems would become the least of your worries.

Doubt and ambiguity must be erased and replaced with clarity, faith, and a deep knowing. As Auntie Pua always says, "When you *know* it, you own it."

Telepathy:
Accessing your Psychic Potentials

All things in the universe, including our thoughts, have "shadowy bodies" that the *kāhuna* call *aka* cords, which we discussed earlier. The *aka* substance is sticky and elastic and can cross any distance, unlimited by space or time. Remember that thoughts, feelings, and *mana* travel along these cords. Among their many lessons, the *kāhuna* teach that illness and distortion of any kind result from interference with the natural flow of the energy that comes from our source. Kāhuna belive that this means all symptoms are a form of conversion reaction, that is, of an emotional, mental, or spiritual imbalance that has taken physical form. Put simply, this means you are able to communicate with others without the direct use of your senses.

This form of communication is achieved through the Lower Self. In principle, this is a relatively simple four-step process:

1. Focus your attention on the person you want to contact.

2. Build up a surplus of *mana.*

3. Hold clearly in your mind the thought you want to transmit.

4. Will the thought on its way.

The unconscious has the strange and marvelous ability to project a portion of its shadowy body across miles through the *aka* cords. This is the same telepathic ability that makes astral travel possible, projecting our whole consciousness over great distances, allowing us to be aware of events hundreds or even thousands of miles away. The primary difference between telepathy and astral travel is in how much of the low shadowy self is projected across the miles. With telepathy we may only project words or thoughts; with astral travel we project our whole consciousness (Steiger 1997).

Changing Your Future

Brad Steiger contends that according to the *kāhuna*, "the Higher Self makes our future from our averaged thoughts, which it picks up during sleep" (1997).

Our future thus unfolds from a hit-and-miss jumble of contrary events, good and bad luck. Because we change our minds so often, sometimes many times every day, it is no wonder that our Higher Self has difficulty finding clear directions for the future. Only if we decide what we want and hold to the decision strongly, working always in one direction, can the Higher Self know the thought forms that we want it to follow to build our desired future.

It is a bit like getting jelly to set . . . you must not stir it!

Lessons in Love

A few years ago, I fell in love with a European man who came to one of my seminars. His first words to me were, "I want to apologize for being a few minutes late last night, but I was with the *kahuna*."

"*Kahuna?*" I asked. "That is my lineage also."

To make a long story short, we ended up having a very intriguing long-distance relationship. We would often meet in wonderful places such as Italy, Spain, or Santa Fe. We seemed to always have that *kahuna* bond, and I was sure we had been together long ago on the Hawaiian Islands. But one year he vanished, right after proposing to me, which he probably didn't remember because, as I recall, he couldn't look me in the face. He proposed to the wind on a terrace facing the palace in Old Madrid. Right after that I lost track of him for the next five years. I never understood this fully but also never felt victimized by it because, obviously, we both created what had occurred, for whatever reason.

A past life with him in Hawai'i came up in a recent regression. I wasn't planning to look at that life, especially after so many years. But Jackie, a new friend of mine, was demonstrating her work to me, and I gladly volunteered. In this past life, I was a *kahuna* who had been in training a long time. It was time for my initiation; I had to demonstrate my ability to change the weather. I stood at the top of the hill and the people were all waiting for me to give them instructions. A deadly tidal wave was coming and we had to turn it back. I was in a state of absolute certainty and my instructions to the people were very clear. It worked perfectly.

My "prize" for this accomplishment was to be married to this very man, my European lover. The trouble was that there was another woman in the picture, one who was very jealous that I was to be betrothed to him. She tried to stop us from getting together by spreading terrible (and false) rumors about me. I had a weak moment of fear that she was in fact going to ruin everything, and instead of staying in my center, and in my certainty, I bought into the drama. And so it happened just as I feared: I lost the chance to marry this man and apparently I had just one chance, as he then disappeared. Having recalled this incident from my past life, it was now clear to me that I had recreated this past life event.

Interestingly enough, this same man just recently reappeared in my life. Could it have anything to do with this greater clarity about why we were in each other's lives?

Absolute certainty is the state of a master *kahuna*. But this certainty cannot be achieved with the ego. There's the test!

The Art and Science of Manifesting

Manifestation is a simple science to the *kāhuna*—and yet, this is knowledge that could revolutionize the world. To a *kahuna*, manifestation is a relaxed and effortless endeavor that follows these ten steps:

1. State firmly what you want when you are in a happy, clear mood.

2. Hold your concentration on the goal with a clear picture. See it in your mind's eye, and do not change the picture while working with it.

3. Release all resistance and negativity within yourself, and commit to the picture you are holding in your mind's eye.

4. Make sure that what you are picturing does not affect other people.

5. Feel that you already have what you are visualizing and that you are living in that state of being. For example, if you are manifesting money, imagine how you would feel in this moment if you already had it.

6. Gather *mana* by deep breathing.

7. Ask for your Lower Self's cooperation in bringing the *mana* to your Higher Self in order to realize your goal.

8. Never question how it will be given to you, and never doubt that it will come to you.

9. Do not tell anyone else what you are working on. When you tell others who are not supportive, their negative feelings and doubts can affect the outcome in a negative way.

10. Know that the universe contains an infinite supply of everything you need and that you can draw it to you at this time (Berney 2000).

Remember that breath is the fuel of prayers. Deep breathing done with intention, slowly and consciously, gathers *mana*. Then the *mana* is offered to the Higher Self for a specific stated purpose, producing directed *mana*.

In regard to prayer in general, the *kāhuna* say that when wise guidance is needed, apply in prayer to the Father. Turn to the Mother for supply. When changes in your present circumstances are needed, apply in prayer to both Father and Mother, asking them to work together to create the desired outcome.

You may receive daily contact and hourly guidance

from the Higher Self if you ask for it. But the Higher Self will not interfere with what you are doing, regardless of how you may be muddling up your life, unless you ask it to come to your aid (Long 1948).

Asking opens doors!

Australian Spirituality

I received such a huge blessing immediately after completing this section of the book: Gerry Bostock came to see me. He is the real thing, an aboriginal healer, or medicine person, from the Bundjulung Tribe, trained from the age of three. He is the Australian version of a Hawaiian *kahuna*.

I had wanted Gerry to come over and charge up a crystal I had purchased at the Tucson Gem Show. He is, after all, a master healer with crystals. I told my assistants to hang around, as I knew they would enjoy meeting him. He walked in, looking exactly how you would imagine an Aboriginal healer to look: bearded and deeply tanned, with soft facial features and piercing eyes.

"I just came back from a house call in Alaska," he said.

"Oh," I said. "What was the condition?"

"Constipation" he said casually.

I loved talking shop with Gerry, and I encouraged my Australian breathworkers and my acupuncturist to listen while he told us about his latest products.

He is now producing two new products from native plants that only aborigines know about. One is called Kudjulak, which he says is a heart cream that helps conditions of the heart. It is also, as he explained enigmatically, about women's business, to be applied to the vagina. The other product is WiJin WiJin, or "old man healer," for stiff or sore muscles and bones. This cream was penetratingly hot. I told him I hoped I didn't get the two creams mixed up! He showed me the dot at the bottom of one of the jars to ease my mind.

Gerry explained how he had prepared the herbs ever so carefully, growing them with crystals, talking to the plants, and doing high ceremonies to prepare the plants for their purpose. The "coding" he had given them would go into the body.

Gerry told me how his ancestors, many of whom were out-of-the-body at the time, trained him. It reminded me so much of what I had read about the Hawaiian *kāhuna*. They always acknowledged their ancestors. Gerry said that these out-of-the-body ancestors had "downloaded" so much to him that some of it had not even begun to get to him until he was well into the eighties. I told him I hoped my master

Babaji was downloading more healing knowledge for me so that I could use it in the future.

"Yes," he said, "that is the way it works."

Of course I was hoping he would give me a massage with the creams, but that wasn't the reason I had called for him. I told him that my shoulder was sore from a small bike accident. He reminded me that there was no such thing as an accident, that it was just the body's way of getting me to recognize what I had not addressed.

I agreed and told him I knew exactly what the issue was. I needed better discernment, faster.

Gerry told me to get ready, quite eager to try the creams on me. I told my acupuncturist, Vicki, that she could watch, as I knew he would teach her a lot. He went over every detail of my body, telling Vicki exactly how to clear ligaments the aboriginal way. At one point he told her to go to the living room and bring him the gold cloth. He laid it over me, and I knew he had charged it up just like the *kahuna* did in Hawai'i.

After one hour of TLC (which he said I needed more of) with these marvelous creams, he suddenly started shouting that it was definitely a past life. He showed me where a spear had gone into my body and out the other side. I hadn't told him any details of what I remembered in an earlier breathwork session that had revealed this past life. I was tied up in that life at the end and could not get the spear out, so

I eventually bled to death. Gerry already knew this, as he suddenly started tying tea towels around my wrists and pulling on my arms, holding them out and recreating the scene of my fatal wounds.

The lesson I was to receive was about self-sabotage and how it led to my death in that past life. Following the session with Gerry, I was reminded that the *kāhuna* say we should always be happy, even for misfortune, for with misfortune comes wisdom that we could not have otherwise received. And that is the gift in misfortune. Every trial is an opportunity to examine oneself and work out any negativity that may have crept into our consciousness. Introspection is crucial.

Following my session, I told Gerry that I had gone to the Vagina Cave on the Big Island after having met him on Maui. Then I told him the name of this book.

"I have a story for you," he said, sitting down and making himself comfortable. He told us a story about a patient he had worked on in Kona, a town on the Big Island. The patient had had an inoperable brain tumor. Gerry and another healer worked on her a lot before he got the idea to have his patient ask Madame Pele to assist. He told the patient that she would need to make an offering to Pele. The only thing the woman had was an expensive gold cross. The ceremony began. Gerry put crystals in a glass of water. He took the crystals out and had the woman drink most of the water. Then she threw the cross up in the air and out to sea, offering it to Pele.

Traditionally, offerings of this kind are made directly to the volcano, since Pele is the goddess of fire. However, it is safe to say that Pele received the gift because they all saw the cross disappear in midair and never fall into the ocean. Instantly, the remaining liquid in the glass turned magenta. Then the glass broke so nobody else could ever use it.

I naturally wanted to know the result of this healing with Pele. Gerry said that the last he had heard, when the doctors did a CAT scan they saw a strange liquid around the tumor that was eating it away!

After our long visit, I asked Gerry to teach with me at my next seminar. Vicki reminded me that my last night in Australia, upon my return from New Zealand, would be the very night that Mars would get as big as the moon. It would be the closest Mars had been to the earth in eighty thousand years. I was reminded that in India they say there is nothing higher than worship of the Divine Mother. I asked Gerry to join us in our ceremonies to the Divine Mother on the night when Mars would shine like the moon.

A Maori Healing, *Kahuna* Style

I was in New Zealand teaching about ways to honor the Divine Mother. On my birthday I told the gathering that what I wanted more than anything else was to meet with some Maori elders, who were traditional healers in their own culture, similar to the *kāhuna* in Hawai'i. At this time we discovered they were in other parts of New Zealand. Undaunted, my organizers, Pete and Pauline, spent all morning making calls to successfully locate elders who were in Wellington.

We discovered they were at an old hospital the government had given over to Te Whanau Kotahi Ora, a Maori Rongoa Traditional Healing Center. I was led to the back room of the hospital, where chairs were lined up against the walls. Usually, just like in Hawai'i, everyone would sit around watching and waiting for their turn. But we were lucky—everyone was gone and we had the whole place to ourselves.

I was taken to Teawhina Reiwaka, a large Maori woman who greeted me by name and said she had been waiting for me. She immediately hooked me up to some coils she explained were charged up by special white rocks.

Teawhina Reiwaka chanted over me and then, after the treatment with the rocks, gave me an unusual chiropractic adjustment on my head. Then her assistant gave me a special massage. Teawhina was fascinated with her new cell phone, which had a digital camera in it. She took my picture and told me how honored they were that I was visiting. She took me to the herb room to meet her husband, who was in charge of the herbs. This Maori healer was a real character, and I liked her a lot. She seemed to be working on me on a lot of different levels.

> She walked into my room looking like an angel. She sang Maori chants over me and did prayers. She said she had to remove one entity and extract a spear from a past life.

But then I got even luckier. That night in my hotel room I had a surprise visit from another Maori healer. I didn't even know she was coming. Word had gotten around, she said. She walked into my room looking like an angel. She sang Maori chants over me and did prayers. She said she had to remove one entity and extract a spear from a past life.

She told me the elders were in the room, as was my Swedish grandfather. She said that one of the elders was going to stick around with me. She left me in a very high state. I was in bliss for over an hour. It was my last night in New Zealand. What a blessing. What a birthday.

Spirituality in Everyday Life

Kāhuna are experts in a great variety of fields, particularly in spiritual development and healing. As with other native cultures and backgrounds that I've become familiar with, I feel particularly in tune with the Huna practice, as it is all about using the power of the mind to create reality. It is also about savoring existence joyfully while experiencing all that we can be. Huna offers a process for getting all parts of ourselves in agreement through effective prayer, methods for conflict resolution, ways for clearing emotional blocks, and many other benefits that will come naturally as we bring these practices into our lives.

You can learn to create complete happiness and success with Huna. You can learn to be your own *kahuna* now and even become your own spiritual advisor. Max Freedom Long, the great researcher of Huna philosophy, once said that if you are not using Huna, you are working too hard.

Imagine how society would change if we all worked to remove harmful patterns from our lives and if we truly understood the power of our own energy, or *mana*. We could gather *mana* to heal ourselves, for example.

The use of breath is the heart of Huna practice. So it works hand-in-hand with the Sacred Renewal Breathwork that I do. We can all become *kāhuna* now and create magic. The secrecy of it all is a thing of the past.

Waiho Wale Kahiko—ancient secrets are now revealed.

Reflections on Immortality

My encounters with Madame Pele raised many extraordinary questions in my mind. I was brought back time and again to the question of immortality. Being an Immortalist, I have studied this subject for many years and have taught it to others. I started thinking that if she, Pele, is all about the passion for life, and if life is eternal and we are all life, then why is everyone saying that death is inevitable? Most people think that death is beyond our control. Some believe it is caused by God or that Satan is to blame. Others simply blame it on "nature," claiming that, of course, it is natural to die. But when you are watching a volcano erupt and you see how life keeps reappearing, you start thinking about how life continues. Something doesn't add up there. If we believe that God causes death, then aren't we making God out to be a murderer?

Pele herself is the very essence of the creative impulse of the universe, which itself is immortal. Some people will look at Pele's eruptions and think of her as a destructive force, but in fact, that is wrong. Those people do not know the full story. As Auntie Pua has told me many times: "When people say Pele is a destroyer . . . no! She is reclaiming the land. This is her *kuleana,* her responsibility. She is the menstrual cycle of our planet. She reclaims land that has been desecrated, and with the flow of her lava she gives back new land. People have strayed away from understanding all this about who she is." In so many different ways, Pele teaches us to honor the endless cycles of life—creation and destruction—and the continuation of the life force through all of it.

Many spiritual paths do not take into consideration that ascension and physical immortality are the ultimate goals of spiritual development and growth. You have to keep dying and reincarnating to step out of the birth-death cycle. The problem is that most people are stuck in a comfort zone beyond which they do not wish to move. They don't realize that this zone is very uncomfortable compared to where they could evolve to with the understanding of ascension and physical immortality.

On one of my trips to India, years before my visits to Pele and the Vagina Cave, a stranger handed me an article titled "The Last Initiation." It was on the subject of physical immortality and ascension. I regret that I cannot tell you the name of the author, as none was given on the article and my attempts to identify who wrote it have been unsuccessful. Nevertheless, the following sentence leapt out at me: "Finally, the concept of immortality implies a harmonization of the entire personality and transformation of the physical organism as an effective channel of expression of higher values."

In the history and legends of the Huna tradition, there are many stories about immortality and what it means to one day take on a spiritual form, one where you are completely invulnerable. Cataclysmic events will not harm an ascended being on earth, as you will be able to instantaneously beam to any area of safety. You will have a light body that will dwell multi-dimensionally.

Consider the miracle of life and remember that your life is a miracle: Maybe all we really need to do is stop killing ourselves with our *belief in death*. What if you got out of the hypnotic state of social trance that you accepted from others as you were growing up? What if you actually disengaged from the collective consciousness that believes in aging and dying? What if you could experience union with God while still in your body? What if you continued to regenerate the cells of your body? What if you could activate the Christ Codes in yourself?

Of course, I am talking here about immortal enlightenment, that is, our awakening to the very real possibility of physical immortality. One thing is clear: This whole planet is ascending and you have chosen to be here at this miraculous time, when you can consciously assist every cell of your body to receive the highest light frequencies. This is the gift of immortal enlightenment that is being offered. The gift is that life is everlasting regardless of how many times the body dies. In other words, the soul does live on and creates a new body for itself if you reincarnate. It is also true that your soul is endowed with wisdom, and it knows that death of the body is out of harmony with the universal law of life. Your soul yearns to be exalted by the vibration of the ascension attitudes so that it can travel the way of the already ascended masters.

After your ascension, you can choose to return as an ascended master in an immortal light body with the ability to dematerialize and rematerialize at will. You will be able to perform miracles and create spontaneously out of the etheric substance. Being in the ascended state, you will not be affected by negativity, doubt, fear, financial worries, and other sorts of limitations. Veils will be lifted from you—you can be free, radical, and outrageous! Upon your ascension you will attain a more youthful age. If you are a healer, you will be able to channel much more healing energy and heal spontaneously.

Why postpone what is so blissful and so liberating? The joy and love an ascended master has to offer is far beyond what you have so far experienced. There is a huge smorgasbord of delight awaiting you. Once you ascend you do not have to die. At any time you desire you can rematerialize. You are not giving up your body. You are evolving it.

The subject of physical immortality is a complex and fascinating one that has profound implications for everyone living on the planet at this time. But there is hardly space in this book to cover this subject in the manner it deserves. That will be another book, and I'm happy to tell you that it is already a work in progress, beginning to take on a life of its own, so perhaps by the time you have read *Pele's Wish* this next book will be ready for you.

Completing a Journey

When I landed on Maui, I was looking forward to saturating my soul with the Divine Mother Energy of the island and finishing this book. One of the first things that happened was my organizer, Diana, handed me a magazine called *ZENTO*. I just love magazines . . . even won an award in grade school for selling the most door to door. I opened the magazine straight to an article titled "A Love Affair of a

Different Kind." And guess what it was about: Pele! Well, it was really about a volcano man named Brad Lewis, who makes his living capturing the essence of creation that Pele expresses. He photographs the raw power and beauty of the volcanoes. Lewis himself lives on the summit of Kīlauea Volcano. Over the past twenty years, he has spent day and night in the warm embrace of Pele, tent pitched and cameras at hand, ready to capture her amazing dance of creation.

Lewis admits that the dangers are extreme at times. He often smells the rubber on his shoes melting. Because of the way he is supporting science, he obviously has a ticket to go beyond the "no trespassing" signs and enter into the most intimate spaces with Pele. He says on his website: "Nowhere else on Earth is creation happening on a continual basis at such a rapid rate." Well, if you look at the photographs it seems like Pele is posing for him.

My roommate, Jaye, a cranial therapist, walked past where I had the magazine open. "Is that lava formed as a heart?" she asked.

"Exactly," I said.

Lewis captures the different forms that Pele makes when shooting lava into the sky. He states: "There are too many things that I've seen that are too unbelievable to go anywhere but the spiritual realm of the creative Pele energy."

Through his photos, Lewis allows us to see a world

that is otherwise inaccessible. How could we comprehend the bigger picture of the Divine Mother?

The Earth is alive!

Are you doing your part to support that truth?

Well, that is Pele's wish.

Pele herself is going to be whispering in your ear . . .

To you with love,
Sondra Ray

A Glossary of Terms in Native Hawaiian

Ho'o maika'i—the skill of blessing

Pikopiko—the skill of energizing power centers

Ike-papalua—the skill of shifting to another level of awareness

Noho—the skill of channeling

Ka'ao—the skill of storytelling

Kahi—the skill of healing with dual focus

Ho'omanamana—the skill of empowerment

Kaulike—the skill of balancing/integrating the body

Hailona—the skill of tuning into the past, present, and future

La'akea—the skill of energizing and healing *aka* fields

Haipule—the skill of manifesting events and circumstances

Kulike—the skill of shape-shifting

Mo'ike—the skill of interpreting dreams

Makaku—the skill of creative dreaming

Komo po—the skill of shamanic journeying

Kimana—the skill of increasing personal energy

Nalu—the skill of contemplative manifestation

Kalana hula—the skill of focused movement

Ho'ailona—the skill of healing with symbols and omens

Hana la'a—the skill of ritual and ceremony

Kuhikuhipu'u'one—the skill of geomancy

Hele kihilo—the skill of time travel

Kahoaka—the skill of magical flight

Kukulu kumuhana—the skill of working with group energy
(Found on the wall of a bunkhouse on a permaculture tropical fruit orchard in Pahao, Puna, Hawai'i, September 2003, by Millennium Twain)

Annotated References

The following five books are excellent resources for learning more about traditional Hawaiian cultures and spiritual ways. Beneath each title is a brief description of what the book is about and why you may find it interesting.

Change We Must: My Spiritual Journey, by Nana Veary, Institute of Zen Studies, 1989.

This is Nana's spiritual memoir of how her family helped to set her early course in life. As she recalls her journey, Nana weaves together images and stories that reveal metaphysical truths. From her story we begin to understand ways her teachings can be applied in our everyday lives.

Hawaiian Dictionary (revised and enlarged edition), by Mary Kawena Pukuʻi and Samuel H. Elbert, University of Hawaiʻi Press, 1986.

This definitive work on the Hawaiian language contains more than thirty thousand entries. Much more than a dictionary, it also contains guidelines for pronouncing Hawaiian words and phrases. What makes this book particularly appealing is that it contains folklore, poetry, and ethnology that give the study of the language color and interest. If you wish to expand your knowledge of the

Hawaiian language and culture, this reference book is a must-have.

Ho'oponopono: Contemporary Uses of a Hawaiian Problem-Solving Process, by E. Victoria Shook, University of Hawai'i Press, 1986.

If my discussions of *ho'oponopono* interested you, you'll find this an excellent resource for learning more and applying these skills in a meaningful way. *Ho'oponopono,* which means "to make right," is an excellent healing and conflict resolution method that can help with everything from bringing harmony into a difficult family situation to working with communities. This is considered to be the classic text on the subject and includes core teachings for improving all human relationships.

Nana I Ke Kumu: Look to the Source, by Mary Kawena Puku'i, E. W. Hertig, M.D., and Catherine Lee, Hui Hanai Queen Lili'uokalani Children's Center, 1972.

Mary Kawena Puku'i, author of the *Hawaiian Dictionary,* died in 1986. She was one of Hawai'i's most highly respected and loved historians and authors, in addition to being a musical composer and authority on hula. In this book, she and her co-authors discuss the cultural practices, concepts, and beliefs of Hawai'i. Though this book is out of print, used copies are still available through the

Internet. For anyone interested in early Hawaiian culture, legends, and practices, this book is well worth searching for and reading.

Tales from the Night Rainbow: The Story of a Woman, a People, and an Island, by Koko Willis and Pali Jae Lee, Night Rainbow Publishing, 1986.

The wisdom teachings of early Hawaiian spirituality were contained in stories shared with others through oral storytelling. In this book, the authors present an oral history as told by Ka'iliohe Kame'ekua of Kamalo, Moloka'i. This excellent little book gives you a sense of how early Hawaiians communicated their ideas, not as mere facts but in terms of stories about gods, goddesses, the elements, and their interactions with humans.

References

Berney, C. 2000. *Fundamentals of Hawaiian Mysticism.* Freedom, Calif.: Crossing Press.

Bishop Museum, As told by Dietrich Varez and Pua Kanakaole Kanahele 1991, Reprinted in 1993. *Pele: The Fire Goddess.* Honolulu, Hawaii: Bishop Museum Press.

Kane, Herb Kawainui 1987. *Pele: Goddess of Hawaii's Volcanoes,* Expanded Edition. Captain Cook, Hawaii: The Kawainui Press.

King, S. 1983. *Kahuna Healing: Holistic Health and Healing Practices of Polynesia.* Wheaton, Ill.: Quest Books.

————. 1990. *Urban Shaman: A Handbook for Personal and Planetary Transformation Based on the Hawaiian Way of the Adventurer.* New York: Fireside.

Kupihea, M. 2001. *Kahuna of Light: The World of Hawaiian Spirituality.* Rochester, Vt.: Inner Traditions Inter-national.

Long, M. F. 1948. *The Secret Science behind Miracles: Unveiling the Huna Tradition of the Ancient Polynesians.* Camarillo, Calif.: DeVorss Publications.

————. 1955. *Growing into Light.* Camarillo, Calif.: DeVorss Publications.

————. 1965. *The Huna Code in Religions: The Influence of the Huna Tradition on Modern Faith.* Camarillo, Calif.: DeVorss Publications.

————. 1978. *Recovering the Ancient Magic.* Cape Girardeau, Mo.: Huna Research, Inc.

Pukui, M. K., and S. H. Elbert. 1986. *Hawaiian Dictionary.* Rev. ed. Honolulu: University of Hawai'i Press.

Pukui, M. K., E. W. Hertig, and Catherine Lee. 1972. *Nana I Ke Kumu: Look to the Source.* Hawai'i: Hui Hanai Queen Lili'uokalani Children's Center.

Shook, E. V. 1986. *Ho'oponopono: Contemporary Uses of a Hawaiian Problem-Solving Process.* Honolulu: Univer-sity of Hawai'i Press.

Steiger, B. 1997. *Kahuna Magic.* Atglen, Pa.: Schiffer Pub-lishing.

Stone, J. D. 1997. *Hidden Mysteries: Ets, Ancient Mystery Schools and Ascension.* Flagstaff, Ariz.: Light Technol-ogy Publishing.

Veary, N. 1989. *Change We Must: My Spiritual Journey.* Honolulu: Institute of Zen Studies.

Willis, K., and P. J. Lee. 1986. *Tales from the Night Rainbow: The Story of a Woman, a People, and an Island.* Hawaii: Night Rainbow Publishing.

About Rebirthing

Rebirthing was started in 1974. It is a powerful breathing process done with a breath coach. Through "conscious connected breathing," you receive more life force energy than you would normally. As this force flows through you, it brings awareness to all the areas in the body/mind that are blocked for the purpose of release. It brings the unconscious to the conscious without drugs or hypnosis, so that one can change sabotaging thoughts and patterns. It helps clear psychosomatic ailments. It helps clear relationships and sexual issues, and it opens you up when you feel stuck or shut down. It is emotional release work. It helps release traumatic birth memories or past lives. It accelerates your growth immensely and gives you a divine experience. It helps rejuvenate the body and purifies death programming. It is the fastest purification method I have ever used.

Over the years, many rebirthers have improved and updated the work. In Sacred Renewal Breathwork, I have added other spiritual practices toward the end of the session to help the client go to the highest vibration possible. Prayers, mantras, and chants of the Divine Mother help to create even more restoration, regeneration, renewal, and ecstasy.

For information on rebirthing worldwide:

The New York and Philadelphia Rebirthing Center
c/o Tony Lo Mastro
1027 69th Avenue
Philadelphia, PA l9126
Phone: (215) 924-6806
E-mail: tony.lomastro@verizon.net

**If you are interested in learning more about *ho'opono-
pono* contact:**

Mabel Katz
Phone: (877) 262-7470
E-mail: Makangel@aol.com
Web: www.MabelKatz.com
Web: www.hooponopono.org

About the Author

Sondra Ray, a pioneer of the rebirthing movement, is a teacher, seminar leader, and devoted student of spiritual disciplines. Her books include *The Only Diet There Is, Healing and Holiness,* and *I Deserve Love.* She lives in Marina del Rey, CA.

For information on Sondra Ray:
Web: www.SondraRay.com
E-mail: See calendar page of website.
India trip information given on website.

Puanani Mahoe shares the teachings of Hawaiian spirituality through lectures, blessings, and *ho'oponopono* gatherings. A frequent guest on radio and television, she is a graduate of Kamehameha Schools on O'ahu and currently resides on Maui.